Timeless Truths from a Faithful Shepherd

Landmark Sermons from the Teaching Ministry of

Steven A. Kreloff

30th Anniversary Anthology
1981 – 2011

Copyright © 2011 by Steven A. Kreloff

Timeless Truths from a Faithful Shepherd
Landmark Sermons from the Teaching Ministry
of Steven A. Kreloff
by Steven A. Kreloff

Printed in the United States of America

ISBN 9781612156071

All rights reserved solely by the author. The author guarantees all contents are original and do not infringe upon the legal rights of any other person or work. No part of this book may be reproduced in any form without the permission of the author. The views expressed in this book are not necessarily those of the publisher.

Unless otherwise indicated, Bible quotations are taken from The New American Standard Bible ®. Copyright © 1960, 1962, 1963, 1968, 1971, 1972, 1973, 1975, 1977, 1988, and 1995 by The Lockman Foundation, and are used by permission.

www.xulonpress.com

6-19-11

Richard,

Pastor Kreloff is a Jewish Christian who has a pretty little church & it reminds me very much of Immanuel, in Clearwater.

This book is a collection of some of his most memorable sermons. I hope you enjoy it. Happy, Healthy Father's Day!

Love,
Marilyn

CONTENTS

Foreward ix

Brook Bible Institute 13
December 23, 1984

A Jewish Queen in a Pagan Palace 38
January 19, 1986

How to Have God's Peace 58
August 20, 1989

The Spiritual Marathon 73
February 14, 1993

God Who Comforts the Depressed 98
August 11, 2002

The Believer's Relationship to the Law 124
October 26, 2003

Blessed Are Those Who Mourn 149
January 9, 2005

Christ Our Advocate 175
September 6, 2009

Testing the Spirits 190
September 5, 2010

This book is a collection of a mere handful of the more than 2,100 sermons which Steven A. Kreloff has preached during his 30 years of ministry as the Pastor-Teacher of Lakeside Community Chapel in Clearwater, Florida. No collection which is so limited can adequately represent the depth and breadth of his ministry.

His emphasis on verse-by-verse exposition of the Scriptures has been the nexus for the spiritual birth and growth of hundreds, many of whom are now engaged in full-time ministry. He has taught the Scriptures in both church and educational settings on four continents, and has previously authored two books.

But of greatest importance is his character. He is committed to obeying the Word in his ministry as a local church pastor, in his family life, and in his personal walk with Christ. Truly, he has proven himself to be a faithful shepherd of God's flock.

With deepest love, respect, and gratitude,

The congregation of Lakeside Community Chapel

May 1, 2011

Foreword

I still vividly remember the first time I heard Steve Kreloff preach. It was one of his very earliest sermons—a fifteen-minute message in an introductory homiletics class at Moody Bible Institute. Each student was assigned a day to preach a short sermon, and on the days we weren't scheduled to preach, we were supposed to critique the other students' sermons. Everything was fair game for criticism, from the structure and outline of the message to the speaker's tempo, posture, tone, gestures, and clothing. As you might imagine, student critics can be merciless.

Steve and I had spent hours together doing personal evangelism on the streets of Chicago, and we had already developed a close friendship that still endures (if anything, it's stronger than ever) almost forty years later. But at the time, neither of us had done much preaching. I had certainly never heard Steve preach.

I have to confess that when Steve's turn came to preach in that class, my expectations were low. As much as I loved and respected him for his evangelistic energy and his passion for the gospel, he seemed to lack the vocal and physical apparatus one normally associates with great preachers. He was thin and frail-looking, with a voice more gentle than commanding. Furthermore, Steve and I had spent hours discussing various knotty doctrinal issues, and I was familiar with his approach to solving theological conundrums and interpreting the hard passages of Scripture. He would consider the text from every conceivable angle, meticulously pondering every possible interpretation. He would experiment in his mind with several different points of view until (sometimes after what seemed a very long time) he would finally settle on one. In those days, I might have said his besetting sin was overscrupulousness. He was (and still is) a perfectionist, especially when dealing with vital points of doctrine or biblical interpretation.

So I more or less expected Steve to be timid, nervous, and indefinite in the pulpit. I was braced for the worst.

But Steve's first sermon astonished me, convicted me, taught me, and motivated me. His profound gifts as a preacher, teacher, and biblical exegete were already evident. He spoke with incredible poise and conviction. His content was clear, detailed, accurate, easy to follow—and about as thorough as it's humanly possible to be in 15 minutes. There was not a wasted word or misplaced gesture in Steve's delivery. It was a powerful message, and feedback from the professor and other students emphatically affirmed that assessment.

I came away with a new appreciation for Steve's ultra-attentive approach to the biblical text—and an unshakable conviction about his calling to be a pastor. I've learned more about preaching from watching him and listening to him than I ever did from all my textbooks, homiletics professors, and student critics combined. In no way does that diminish the value of textbooks and professors; but there's no denying that a living example is exceedingly more helpful.

For more than 35 years, no one in my life has been a better example of consistent, faithful, effective ministry than Steve Kreloff. I could see clearly in that first sermon that that the Lord had given Steve a unique gift and a discerning heart. I knew even then that his life and ministry would be blessed and that he would be a blessing to anyone who sat under his teaching. What I did not foresee was that the Lord would call Steve back to the church where he was baptized, and bless the congregation at Lakeside with thirty uninterrupted years of ministry under Steve as senior pastor. For a young pastor to stay so long in one place of ministry is a remarkable achievement, all too rare nowadays.

Steve's preaching for thirty years (and longer) has been marked by the same characteristics that astonished me so much the first time I heard him preach: thoroughness, clarity, meticulous care, deep passion, and firm conviction—delivered in an engaging, earnest, accessible style you could listen to for hours.

I'm glad these messages have been assembled in this form and put into print. Reading them, you'll appreciate their meaty simplicity in a whole new way. These sermons also show the amazing breadth of Steve's knowledge of God's Word. He is as skilled and comfortable in Moses' Law and the book of Esther as he is in a familiar passage like the Beatitudes. And whether you're already familiar with a given text or not, Steve will always show you fresh insights.

The congregation at Lakeside Community Chapel in Clearwater is profoundly blessed to have Steve as their teaching pastor, and I am likewise blessed to have him as a lifelong friend. Congratulations to him and to the people of Lakeside on this thirtieth anniversary of his installation as senior pastor. "May our Lord Jesus Christ Himself and God our Father, who has loved us and given us eternal comfort and good hope by grace, comfort and strengthen your hearts in every good work and word" (2 Thessalonians 2:16-17).

Phil Johnson
Executive Director, Grace to You

Chapter 1

BROOK BIBLE INSTITUTE
1 Kings 17:1-7
December 23, 1984

There is no book of Elijah, but he is written about in 1 and 2 Kings in the Old Testament. He is introduced to us in 1 Kings 17:1-7 which reads as follows:

> *Now Elijah the Tishbite, who was of the settlers of Gilead, said to Ahab, "As the LORD, the God of Israel lives, before whom I stand, surely there shall be neither dew nor rain these years, except by my word." The word of the LORD came to him, saying, "Go away from here and turn eastward, and hide yourself by the brook Cherith, which is east of the Jordan. It shall be that you will drink of the brook, and I have commanded the ravens to provide for you there." So he went and did according to the word of the LORD, for he went and lived by the brook Cherith, which is east of the Jordan. The ravens brought him bread and meat in the morning and bread and meat in the evening, and he would drink from the brook. It hap-*

pened after a while that the brook dried up, because there was no rain in the land.

The prophet Elijah was a man. He wasn't a spiritual superman; he was a man just like us. In fact, that's what it says in James 5 where James emphasizes that Elijah prayed and it didn't rain. Then he says, *"Then he prayed again, and the sky poured rain"* (James 5:18). James wanted his readers to know that Elijah is no different than them; that there is power in prayer. In James 5:17, James says that *"Elijah was a man with a nature like ours"* (James 5:17) which means Elijah is a man who's just like us. There are many legends in Jewish history about Elijah, but the word of God says he's just a man. But the difference is that Elijah, while being just a man, lived on a supernatural level; a level different than most men. The Bible introduces Elijah to us in such a dramatic, abrupt, and forthright fashion that it indicates to us that his life was going to be like that, his ministry was going to be like that—abrupt, dramatic, spectacular, supernatural, and miraculous. That is Elijah's ministry.

Elijah begins his ministry by marching out of the mountains of Gilead and into the palace of Ahab, and he announces, "The Lord God of Israel lives. Not Baal – Baal is no god. Jehovah is the God of Israel, the one true God, and there's going to be neither rain nor dew because Israel is following false gods." That was essentially Elijah's message; very dramatic and very spectacular. With that proclamation, Elijah was thrust into a very public and a very spectacular ministry. In the future, he will rebuke the entire nation of Israel and he will challenge hundreds of false prophets. He will call down fire from heaven on more than one occasion. This man's ministry is unique. It is public, it is spectacular, and it is dramatic. He is called the prophet of fire.

But if we're not careful, that could be all we see about Elijah's ministry. If we're not careful, all we would see when we examine this man's ministry is a series of one spectacular public event after another. All we would see would be Elijah confronting the people, the nation, and the false prophets. All we would see is a man who is in the battle, who's in the forefront, who's on the battlefield in front of everybody. But that's not all there was to Elijah's ministry, and God doesn't want us to have a distorted view of this man's ministry. In fact, maybe that's why so many people feel like they can't relate to Elijah, because all they see is just one spectacular event after another, and so they say, "How can I relate to that guy?" But God doesn't want us to have a distorted view of the man's ministry. He doesn't want us only to see the public confrontations; He also wants us to see the private concealment.

In 1 Kings 17:2-8, God takes us behind the scenes, and He shows us how He prepared Elijah for his future public battles. For Elijah to have an effective public ministry, he had to be trained by the Lord in private, and that is the beauty of this man's ministry. Many people only see him on the battleground, in the field, in the public arena. But there was tremendous training that took place behind the scenes, and it's important that we examine this training period in the life of this man because there are lessons for us to learn from this Old Testament prophet.

In fact, every servant of God, whether an Old Testament prophet or a New Testament child of God, must go through a specific period of private training if he or she is to have an effective public ministry. Many people don't realize that, but that is God's pattern, which we can say with authority. When He chooses a man or a woman to use (which is God's desire for all of us who know the Lord Jesus Christ), He takes that man or woman and He gives them private lessons. He tutors him and He puts him into His own personal Bible Institute.

What do I mean by "Bible Institute"? Well, Joseph received his private schooling in an Egyptian prison, and that was before the time he became a public governor of Egypt. Joseph had to be trained in a pit and in a prison, and then God said, "You're ready now to be publicly used by Me." Only then did he became governor of Egypt.

Moses spent 40 years in a desert before he was ready to lead Israel. For forty years God had to take him to the desert and teach him valuable lessons before he was ready to go back and stand before Pharaoh and say, "Let my people go." Moses was enrolled in the Sinai Bible Institute.

David needed years of private training before he was ready to be the king God wanted him to be. God had chosen him to be the king and God said, "He's the rightful king, not Saul," yet David wasn't ready yet to lead. David was a shepherd, but he needed to learn how to respond to the Chief Shepherd, and so there were several years for David to be trained before he became the king in the public's eye.

Even the great apostle Paul spent three years in Arabia before a public ministry was opened up to him. He was enrolled in the Arabian Bible Institute. The Lord's own disciples were trained by Him for three years before they were ready to be indwelt by the Spirit of God and sent out as missionaries and apostles.

That's the truth with Elijah. Elijah must spend time away from the public eye, alone with God, if he is to carry out an effective ministry. His private training takes place during the three years of drought and famine in Israel, and it takes place in two different locations. The first place was by a brook of water known as Cherith, and the second place was in a Phoenician city north of Israel named Zarephath.

In this message, I want to visit the campus of the Brook Bible Institute or BBI. We want to sit in on a class and observe the initial training, because there's going to be more training after this. But this is the initial training of Elijah as God prepares him for his ministry. We want to look at the three biblical lessons that the Lord has for him: Seclusion

101, Submission 101, and Sustenance 101. These three lessons are lessons that we need to learn as we see principles throughout this passage that we all need to learn and incorporate into our lives. Let's look at the first lesson and the first class: Seclusion 101. Seclusion 101 isn't graduate school; Zarepheth will be the graduate school. Seclusion 101 is just the Bible institute, not seminary. After storming the palace of Ahab and announcing God's judgment to the nation of Israel, the Bible simply says in 1 Kings 17:2-4, *"The word of the LORD came to him, saying, 'Go away from here and turn eastward, and hide yourself by the brook Cherith, which is east of the Jordan. It shall be that you will drink of the brook, and I have commanded the ravens to provide for you there.'"* Now we might pass over this and say, "Well, that's interesting, that's historical, that's accurate, or that's enlightening." But have you ever stopped to realize what must have gone on in Elijah's mind when he heard this? We aren't told specifically what Elijah thought, but I'll tell you what I would have thought if I was him. I would have said, "Look, Lord, do you know what You're talking about? I'm your man for this hour; don't tell me to go away and hide—You must have the wrong person. Can't You see that I'm the only one standing for you." I would have said, "Hide myself? What are you talking about? There's so much work to be done, and there's nobody else to do it. You don't want me to hide, Lord. That must be Your will for someone else. You want me to go and preach; in fact, I'm going to set up a preaching tour and we'll put pressure on Ahab and he'll take down all the false images. Lord, this isn't the time to hide. This isn't the time for me to be secluded. This is the time for me to be out in the open with dramatic messages. Israel needs to hear the Word, which means they don't need me to be hidden away by some brook." I think that's what I would have said. If I didn't say it, I certainly would have thought it.

We aren't told what Elijah said or what he thought, but we are told that God didn't say, "Elijah, it's time to get to work. Elijah, it's time to preach." Rather, He just said, "Hide." That was the command. And the question that we need to ask is, "Why? Why, at such a vital time in Israel's history, does God take the man who stands out and stands up for Him, and say, "Hide, seclude yourself, get away from here." Why? I think there are three basic reasons that God told him to hide. Number one: it was for Elijah's own protection. I don't think this is the primary reason, as God could have protected him in any way He chose to do so, but I think the truth here is that this was for Elijah's own protection. This brook was so desolate and located in such a lonely place that even today with all of our modern scholarship, geographers aren't sure where this brook was located. Even though much is known about Old Testament geography, history, and archeology, it was such an isolated area, no one is sure of its location. But we do know that it was so far away that not even Ahab or his wife Jezebel could find him. So the first reason that God told Elijah to hide is that so He could be protected by God. He could have done it in a number of ways but He chose that way.

The second reason why Elijah was secluded and hidden by God was that it was God's judgment on Israel. I would have said, "Lord, now is the time to speak." But there is a principle in Scripture that when God worked in Israel, when He was judging the nation, many times He withheld His voice. Many times He did that because the one person Israel needed most during this drought was Elijah. They needed to hear the Word of the Lord. They needed God's voice through this prophet, but God was judging Israel and part of the judgment was God's silence. Amos 8:11 brings out this truth: *"Behold, days are coming,"* declares the Lord GOD, *"when I will send a famine on the land, not a famine for bread or a thirst for water, but rather for hearing the words of the LORD."* There are many times in the Old Testament where God withheld His voice through His prophets because He was judging the nation of Israel. Israel had totally disregarded the Word of the Lord and they had followed Baal, the god of the sun. Baal was the false, pagan, Canaanite-Phoenician god, and they had followed him, and now God was giving Israel what they had asked for—silence from Him when they needed Him most. So the second reason was that it was God's judgment on Israel.

But there was another reason (and this is the major reason) why God told Elijah to hide at this brook. God wanted Elijah out of the spotlight—completely out of the spotlight—so He could teach him the one lesson that Elijah needed to learn so that He could communicate to His people. What was that lesson? What was the one lesson Israel needed to know and hear? That the Lord God of Israel lives! God wanted to teach Elijah, in a very unique way, that He was alive and well and could take care of him.

Now you say, "Wait a minute! Elijah knew that! Elijah had his theology right because Elijah announced before Ahab, *'As the Lord, the God of Israel lives...'*(v. 1).Why would God take him aside now to teach him that if he already knew it?" The answer is that it is one thing to know it theologically and it's another thing to experience it. It's one thing to preach the truth; it's another thing for God to set you aside and say, "Let Me teach you the depth of that truth. Let me teach you the reality of that truth." That's what was taking place in Elijah's life. Elijah needed to know that God was alive.

Think what life would be like at that brook. We've got to take ourselves out of the twentieth century, and put ourselves in Elijah's place. Put yourself back in 1Kings 17. What would that brook be like? There were no other humans, no social interaction, no newspapers (the *Jerusalem Post* wasn't flown in daily). Ravens took him food but they didn't bring the newspaper; the *Tel Aviv Tribune* wasn't there. There was no television and no radio; nothing but water from a brook and food flown in by ravens to eat! That was it! I don't think he was there for just a few days. We're not told specifically how long, but it must have been a considerable length of time because there had to have been time for the brook to dry up. Every day it was the same – no humans; only God with whom to have fellowship. Don't you think Elijah got to know the Lord? Don't you think that what he had proclaimed to Ahab became experiential truth for him? *"As the Lord, the God of Israel lives*...and I know He lives." And every time he drank from that brook, and every time the ravens flew in that food, don't you think he was constantly reminded that the God of Israel is alive? He's alive! Every day that Elijah lived was one more demonstration that the God of Israel lived.

Some of you may be beside your own brook these days, and God has sovereignly placed you there. You're out of the spotlight. You'd like to have a ministry; perhaps you'd like to be teaching somewhere. You'd like to be involved in something which makes you feel like you're accomplishing something for God, but you're not. God has taken you aside and hidden you, so to speak. He's done it because He wants to communicate lessons to you that He couldn't or wouldn't communicate if you were in the spotlight. He needs you to sit by your own brook; not necessarily a literal brook, but the brook of seclusion that He has for you because He wants to teach and train you. He's got his own unique Brook Bible Institute where you are enrolled, and it's all part of your training to go through these times of private instruction before you can have an effective public ministry.

You say, "But wait a minute! I know my theology and I don't need to be trained anymore." Elijah knew his theology too; in fact, he was great on theology. He said, *"The Lord, the God of Israel lives."* What better theology is that, especially in a day of apostasy? You may say, "But I already have boldness and courage, why do I need to be trained?" Elijah had courage and boldness too. You don't walk up to the palace of Ahab and Jezebel and speak like he did without some courage. You may say, "But look, I've got the right motivation. I've got the right desires and I want God to be glorified in my ministry." Elijah did too and he was willing to put his whole reputation on the line for God's glory. But still, God put him aside. God put him in Seclusion 101 because the Lord wanted Elijah to know Him deeper. These aren't wasted years that you're secluded. Maybe you were secluded a while back, years ago, and you need a refresher course. There's no age limit to this. These aren't wasted years; these are secluded years. We live in a busy world and there are Christians who want to get busy for God, but what they really need is to let the Lord hide them in His own time, in His own place, and wait for His instructions.

Now I'm not saying there is a time when you don't serve the Lord, so do not take this to mean that we're not to be involved in service. But if you find that God has secluded you, it's for a reason. I thank God for the years I spent in the background as they were years of learning who God is, years of learning that I could depend upon Him to care for me, years of Him sustaining me and letting me know that He could be trusted, years of understanding and learning that His Word—even in the smallest details—is dependable and trustworthy. Those were valuable years. Yes, they were years of obscurity, but they were valuable because I couldn't have handled the work and the pressures of the ministry if I hadn't experienced those years. I've since learned that my experience wasn't unique among pastors. This isn't a message just for pastors or men preparing for the ministry because we're all involved in the ministry, but I have learned that it is not a unique experience exclusive to me.

Alexander McClaren, a Scotsman and one of the finest preachers of the 1800s, said this to a group of young ministers:

I thank God that I was stuck down in a quiet, little obscure place to begin my ministry for that is what spoils half of you young fellows. You get pitch-forked into prominent positions at once and then fritter yourselves away at all manner of little engagements that you call duties instead of stopping at home and reading your Bibles, and getting near to God. I thank God, for the early years of struggle and obscurity.[1]

In my studies and research I have discovered that not only McClaren had that experience, but others like G. Campbell Morgan, Charles Spurgeon, and Joseph Parker endured obscurity for years. What was God doing? He was simply laying the foundation of their ministry. So those are not wasted years. I'm sure there are those who are struggling with this very issue. You're eager to have an effective ministry, which means your heart is in the right place. You are eager to get going but somehow you aren't being used like you feel you should be, and the doors just haven't opened, so you struggle with that and wonder what's going on. Listen: take it from the Lord that it's not the time for you to graduate from the Brook Bible Institute. I don't know when that time is, but it's not your time. In the meantime, use this time wisely; don't struggle with it and don't fight the Lord. Don't tell Him your plans for the great ministry that you want to have, and don't tell Him how wonderful you are, and all the gifts that you have. You can look around and say, "But, Lord, I'm so gifted." Elijah could have said that too. He even said, "But, Lord, there's no one else." God said, "It's alright. Just follow My plan." So use this time wisely by drawing close to the Lord. Use the time to fellowship with Him, and get to know Him well, by studying the Word of God intensely. Don't just study devotions where you don't know what you're reading about; rather, do an intense study and get into the Word. Invest this time wisely in learning the reality of the living God because that is what God wants. You want an effective ministry? Start by getting to know the Lord better. So many people want an instantly mature and well-developed ministry. We live in a world of instant food, instant success, and instant everything, but it just doesn't happen that way in the spiritual arena. Men and women of God aren't made overnight. Most Christians look at Paul's ministry and they say, "What a super guy! Look at what he did! I would love to be going around the world and starting churches and revel in the romance of missionary work." What they forget though is, not only was Paul in the Arabian Desert for a while, but Paul was faithful in a little church in a place called Antioch. In Acts 13, Paul was just one of the elders ministering and serving the Lord, and the Lord looked and saw this faithful man—this man who was in the Word, who was teaching, man who was really, by all measures, hidden and secluded in a little church. In fact, it was the first so-called Gentile church. Although there were both Jews and Gentiles in the congregation, it was the first church which included Gentiles. God said, "Separate Paul and Barnabas for a ministry" (cf. Acts 13:2), and that's what happened. Paul was secluded for a while and God said, "Alright, now is the time." So be faithful where you are, and get to know the Lord. Spend time in His Word, minister where you can, forget about the spotlight, and let God mold you. Part of your education is to learn to accept the seclusion from the Lord. I'm convinced that it is part of the education; to not fight the Lord, but to simply say, "Lord, Your will be done and I'm through struggling. I try to open doors and they close right in my face." Part of the education of seclusion is to accept His dealings in your life even if you can't understand them.

That's what God wanted Elijah to learn, so not only did he give him a class in seclusion, but He also gave him a class in Submission 101. Now, we aren't specifically told what went through Elijah's mind when the word of the Lord came to him and said, "Go hide yourself," but I think it would be a good and proper guess to say that it wasn't the path that Elijah would have chosen had God given him the choice. Why do I say that? Because Elijah was not used to sitting by brooks. Elijah was a robust man, a fiery individual, a rugged mountain man. He wasn't a "brook sitter." Elijah was a fiery prophet, a man with a zealous disposition. Men like that don't usually choose to sit by brooks and let ravens feed them. His nature and temperament weren't the kind that just sat by a brook. But the Bible never says he complained, and it never says he delayed obedience or engaged in arguments with the Lord. I would have argued, but not Elijah.

So what do we learn from this? We learn submission. First Kings 17:5 states, *"So he went and he did according to the Word of the Lord; for he went and lived by the brook Cherith, which is east of the Jordan."* He went without arguing, debating, complaining, or demanding an explanation from the Lord. He submitted to the will of the Lord immediately, even if it was a difficult thing for him to do personally. Part of our training at the Brook Bible Institute is to learn to submit to the Lord even if it's a difficult thing that He tells us He wants us to do. Even if it's something you don't understand, look at Elijah who obeyed and submitted.

Now, I want you to get the picture because this is almost a picture absurdity. It goes against all common sense to tell a grown man to hide himself indefinitely by a brook so that ravens, which were unclean birds, could bring him sustenance. No Israelite was to touch an unclean bird, and yet it is this bird that was going to fly food in to him. Think about that; that sounds absurd, but Elijah did it. You see, sometimes God's Word sounds absurd to us. But when that happens what we need to do is simply submit to it, regardless of how we feel, regardless of whether it goes against our human common sense. We obey and we submit. This is what

God has to teach us before He gives us an effective ministry, because it's all part of the training.

At this point, some may ask, "Why? Why do I have to learn that? Why do I have to learn to do things that don't make sense to me?" Because before you can stand in public and tell others to obey the Word of the Lord, whether it be a salvation message of evangelism to an unsaved person or standing before believers telling them that they must be committed to the Lord, you've got to learn to submit and be committed to the Lord. God doesn't want people running around giving out His message of salvation or demanding a commitment from believers who have never learned to submit themselves. There's no credibility in somebody doing that. You will have people laughing in your face if you tell them that. But don't cop out and say, "That's why I can't be a witness" or "That's good to know because that's why I can't be involved in evangelism; because I haven't learned that." That's a cop out. You learn to submit because that's God's training for you, and if you don't learn, He'll chastise and discipline you. You learn to submit because you cannot have an effective ministry before others unless you learn these lessons in private. How could Elijah stand on the mountain after this private time and say, *"If the Lord is God, then follow Him"* (1 Kings 18:21), without he himself following the Lord? This is what the Lord wanted Elijah to learn. Before he could stand before Israel and command them to obey Jehovah, he first needed to obey Him.

Many of us think that all God wants from us is to learn His Word, and that's a partial truth. But He doesn't just want us to only learn His Word. There are a lot of Christians who have a great deal of knowledge about the Word of God, but that's only part of the picture. He wants us to learn His Word so that we'll obey His Word. It's not a game to learn as much as you can. In fact, 1 Corinthians 8:1 says *"knowledge makes [one] arrogant,"* which simply means that knowing the Bible without obeying it makes you a proud, arrogant, theological egghead. But James1:22 says, *"Prove yourselves doers of the word."* That means you've got to not only hear the Word, but then you've got to do the Word. Jesus said, *"If you continue in my word,"* which means "obedience to God's word," "then *you are truly disciples of mine"* (John 8:31). God wants us to learn the Word so we'll obey and submit to it. You absolutely cannot have an effective ministry, no matter how much knowledge you have, if you aren't obedient and submissive to God's will.

I'm not talking about perfection; rather I'm talking about consistency, which means I'm talking about desire. I'm talking about your heart saying, "I'm submitted to the will of the Lord before I even know what His will is." That's why in the New Testament, God lays down spiritual guidelines in choosing elders and deacons. God doesn't want a leader who hasn't learned first to obey Him, because only those who are themselves submissive to the Lord can speak with any kind of credibility and authority in calling others to submit to the Lord. In fact, Hebrews 13:7 says, *"Remember those who led you, who spoke the word of God to you; and considering the result of their conduct, imitate their faith."*

The first thing the writer to the Hebrews says is this: "I want you to look at your leaders and I want you to see that they have a life that's worth copying; a life of obedient, submissive, faithful leadership." But then he says in verse 17, *"Obey your leaders and submit to them, for they keep watch over your souls as those who will give an account. Let them do this with joy and not with grief, for this would be unprofitable for you."* What's he saying? The first thing he's saying is, "Look, these men are obedient themselves, and since they're obedient, they're the kind of people that you can obey, to whom you can submit." God takes a man and a woman and puts them in an effective, public ministry when they've learned to be obedient, and this learning takes place in private. It's those private lessons; those times behind the scenes where no one else is around but you're learning to submit. You're learning to obey, and you're learning to do what the Lord wants you to do, undergoing those private struggles that no one else knows about. That's what builds character. That's what moves you along in the classroom and in the Bible Institute by the brook.

But there's still one more lesson he needs to learn by the brook and that is his sustenance, or his supply; that is, who sustains him. Elijah needs to learn firsthand that it is God who sustains him. Why is this important? Because the people of Israel didn't look to the Lord to sustain them, rather they looked to the false god, Baal, to sustain them. Let me tell you just a little bit about Baal. He was considered the god of the sun, and as such, he was the one who supposedly gave them the crops that sustained them, which meant that anything they grew or produced was attributed to Baal. Do you see what God has done? God has said, "So you think Baal is the one who can do those things? I'm going to show you who's in charge. See if Baal can produce rain because I'm going to shut the heavens up." God met Baal right at his strength, but in reality there was no Baal. The New Testament tells us that the false gods are simply demons. The point is that the Jewish people, in that day and age, felt that Baal would meet their needs. He would make things grow. He would produce the crops. But it's really Jehovah who's in charge of those things, and God is going to give Elijah a very special lesson on who sustains him. Elijah knew theologically that it wasn't Baal, but he needed to know experientially that it was the Lord. It is one thing to preach, *"My God shall supply all of your needs according to His riches in glory in Christ Jesus,"* (Philippians 4:19), but it is really another thing to prove the reality of that truth. You may believe that, and you may even tell others that God can meet your needs, but you won't be effective if you're not absolutely sure about that yourself. So God has to teach us this lesson, and that's what he's doing with Elijah. The Lord wanted him to have a unique lesson in how He supplied his needs. So 1 King 17:6 says, *"The ravens brought him bread and meat in the morning and bread and meat in the evening, and he would drink from the brook."*

God sustained Elijah in two ways. First, there was the natural way, the natural supply, which was the water from the brook. Second, there was another way by which God supplied Elijah's needs, and that was the supernatural way, whereby the ravens brought him bread and meat in the morning and evening. This is an amazing miracle and we might just pass over this quickly without realizing it. Do you realize that God had to completely change the nature of the ravens to feed Elijah? I don't know much about ravens but I do know this: a raven is a bird that devours large quantities of food. They are greedy and they are known to be gluttonous when it comes to food; in fact, it's where we get our word "ravenous." Someone who is ravenous has a huge appetite; he is gluttonous and has a greedy appetite. But God completely changed the ravens' nature to deliver food because by nature, they would have eaten that food. They don't share with anyone, especially a lone prophet by a brook. God was simply training Elijah to trust him, to depend on Him, to believe His Word, and to obey Him. The Lord wanted Elijah to know that He could and would sustain him in all circumstances. He could stand before the false prophets and not be afraid because he would know that God would sustain him. He could stand before Ahab's soldiers and not be afraid. By the way, he didn't learn the lesson that he could stand before Jezebel and not be afraid; it's another thing when it's a woman! But it shouldn't be another thing. God was teaching him that He sustains him; not to fear anyone else and not to look to anyone else to meet his needs.

Israel was experiencing famine as a result of their sin, but Elijah was eating, and eating well. He didn't have lunch, but he was eating well both in the morning and evening. And he was eating as a result of his obedience! One of the lessons that God must teach us is that He'll supply our needs if we obey! Sometimes we think that we have a blanket promise from the Lord (which we do not) to meet every need. Only obedient Christians have such a promise. For instance, in Matthew 6:33 it says, *"But seek first His kingdom and His righteousness, and all these things will be added to you."* That's a promise with a condition. If you seek first His kingdom and His righteousness, and put Him first in your life, then He'll take care of all the other things. He says, "You don't have to worry like the pagans. You don't have to fret. Your Father in heaven knows what needs you have. You just seek Me first." In Philippians 4:19 it says, *"My God will supply all your needs."* That was given to a very specific people – the Philippians, who were a people who had given of themselves, who had financially given, who had laid down their lives for the brethren. God said to that very generous people, "I'll supply your needs."

Don't get hung up on how God does it. He may use the natural supply, like a job for you to go to, and you'll bring money in that way. The natural supply for Elijah was the brook of water. Elijah still had to scoop it up—it didn't jump out of the brook right into his mouth; he still had to do something. That is the natural, normal way. Most of the time, God operates that way—but not always. He may use some supernatural ways and miracles, like some unexpected ravens. Please understand that I'm not talking literally now, although He could if He wanted to, but God has His supernatural ways of meeting our needs. But the point is that He takes care of those who obey Him; that's the point, and Elijah needed to understand that. Elijah needed to know that He could trust God in every situation. If He could take care of him by a brook with unclean birds and water from that brook, then He could take care of him in any situation. It's so true what the Lord said: if you honor Him, He'll honor you (cf. John 12:26). You can't stand before anyone in public and tell them how wonderful the Lord is and how He can be trusted to meet their needs if you haven't been convinced of that reality. That's so important! God is training you so that you'll know that lesson well. And the sad thing is that many Christians, especially Christian leaders who minister publicly, don't seem to have ever learned that lesson; that God is the One who supplies our needs. They scheme, they plead for money, they write emotionally appealing letters, and that's just not God's way. You look to the Lord to meet your needs, not to others. That doesn't mean you can't tell others your needs at times, it just means don't scheme. Faith is living without scheming. Don't tell them, hoping they'll meet your needs—such as praying in the presence of a rich person—don't do that! You may look very spiritual, but God knows your heart and you know what you're doing. Have you learned that only God sustains you? You live because He says you live and you die because He says you die. Your needs are met because He says your needs are met.

When the Lord Jesus was in the wilderness and He was tempted by Satan, Satan came to Him and said, "Look, if You're the Son of God, why are You starving? Why are You going through this hunger? If You're the Son of God, then turn these stones into bread and eat." Do you know what Jesus said? When He said, *"Man shall not live on bread alone, but on every word that proceeds out of the mouth of God,"* that was not a lesson on, "Let's obey the Bible," even though that is true. We are to obey the Bible, but He wasn't saying we live by obedience. It is a true statement, but that's not what He meant. What He meant was, "Satan, I don't live because of food. Food doesn't sustain Me; God sustains Me. I live because God says I live. When the Word proceeds forth and it says, 'The Son of God lives,' then I live. And when the Word goes forth and it says, 'The Son of God dies,' then I die; not a moment earlier, not a moment later." The Lord Jesus was saying, "God is the One who sustains." I hope you've learned that and I hope I've learned that. We are not to look to people to meet our needs; we are not to scheme, not to connive, but only to look to the Lord. The Lord may use people to meet your needs, but don't look to people to meet your needs; look to the Lord.

Let me give you an example of looking to the Lord to sustain you. I read an illustration in which Howard Hendrix, professor at Dallas Seminary, told the story of how the seminary which was founded in 1924 almost went bankrupt shortly thereafter. He writes,

> All the creditors were ready to foreclose at twelve noon on a particular day. That morning, the founders of the school met in the president's office to pray that God would provide. In that prayer meeting was Harry Ironside.[2] When it was his turn to pray, he said in his refreshingly candid way, "Lord we know that the cattle on a thousand hills are Thine. Please sell some of them and send us the money." Just about that time, a tall Texan in boots and an open-collar shirt strolled into the business office. "Howdy!" he said to the secretary. "I just sold two carloads of cattle over in Fort Worth. I've been trying to make a business deal go through, but it just won't work. I feel God wants me to give this money to the seminary. I don't know if you need it or not, but here's the check," and he handed it over. The secretary took the check and, knowing something of the critical nature of the hour, went to the door of the prayer meeting and timidly tapped. Dr. Lewis Sperry Chafer, the founder and president of the school, answered the door and

took the check from her hand. When he looked at the amount, it was for the exact sum of the debt. Then he recognized the name on the check as that of the cattleman. Turning to Dr. Ironside, he said, "Harry, God sold the cattle."[3]

See, God can supply. God can sustain. You look to the Lord and that's a great lesson God wants us to learn. Whether it takes a babbling brook, some ravens or some cattle, God will sustain you. You need to learn that and I need to learn that. We need to obey Him.

But I want you to know something more serious—even when you do obey the Lord and you look to Him to sustain you, things don't always work out the way you thought they would work out. Things don't always happen in a way that we plan. Look at verse 7: *"It happened after a while that the brook dried up because there was no rain in the land."* The brook dried up. If it had been me, I would have said, "What's going on? I'm in the center of Your will, Lord, and I'm obeying You. I've learned Seclusion 101, I've learned Submission 101, and I'm trying to learn how You sustain me, but now this? The brook dries up!" That's a tough predicament because that's how God has been sustaining Elijah and now it's no more. He can't order in from the local delicatessen so Elijah's in trouble. Why do you suppose God allowed the brook to dry up? It dried up because God wanted to develop the faith of Elijah. You say, "But didn't Elijah learn that God can sustain?" Yes, but apparently he needed to learn more; apparently he needed graduate school. Maybe—and I don't know this with certainty—but maybe Elijah got his eyes off of the Lord and onto the brook. It's very possible for us to get our eyes onto the gifts that God gives us rather than God Himself. I don't really know what was going on in the mind of Elijah, but I know what goes on in our minds. I know what goes on in my mind when my brook runs dry

– "Lord, how can I be in the center of your will and have a dry brook?"

Today, you may be beside a dry brook and you don't know how God is going to meet your needs. I'm not talking only about financial needs; I'm talking about physical, emotional, spiritual, employment, and educational needs. You know you're in the center of His will and you believe that. You know you've done what God wants you to do and yet you don't know where it's going to come from, or when the ravens are going to fly in. And the flesh says, "Panic! Run! Get out of here! Get some outside help—maybe the Lord's forgotten you. Maybe you're not even in His will. Maybe you just thought you were." You begin to doubt and you get frustrated and you wonder if you're really doing what God wants you to do. Do you know what God says about this? He says, "Trust Me. I'm only deepening your faith. I'm only teaching you deeper lessons about sustenance."

Do you want to know why the brook dried up? It's very simple; you don't need a Ph.D. to understand this. He let it dry up because Elijah prayed that it would dry up. Who was the one who prayed that there'd be no rain in Israel? Elijah. God's just answering his prayer. Do you know why some of us are going through some difficult times? Because we have prayed that we would. Haven't you prayed that the Lord would make you a man or woman of God? Mold you to be like Christ? Be conformed to His image? Some of us have prayed, "Lord, give me greater patience," and the Bible says that troubles produce patience (cf. Romans 5:3). God is just answering your prayers. God is saying, "I'm doing what you asked because that is in the will of God." Elijah was right smack in the middle of the will of God and it takes adversity and problems to do that. James 1:2-4 tells us, *"Consider it all joy, my brethren, when you encounter various trials, knowing that the testing of your faith produces endurance. And let endurance have its perfect result, so that you may be perfect and complete, lacking in nothing."* God says, "When the troubles come, don't fight it!" Ask God for wisdom while you're going through it and He'll teach you. He'll teach you the lessons He has for you. The truth of the matter is that the Lord is simply training you in some of the lessons from the Brook Bible Institute. They aren't always easy: the lessons of seclusion, submission, and sustenance. Those were Elijah's lessons and those are the lessons for us because these are the principles and patterns of the Word of God. Do you know what happened when Elijah's brook dried up? God provided another brook for him and a widow who would take care of him. He was promoted to graduate school—that's all. God said to Elijah, "You just watch and wait on Me and I'll give you further instructions as to how I'm going to supply your needs." And that's what God says to us: "Don't run, don't panic; just watch and obey and I'll take care of how everything is supplied. Your concern is simply to pursue righteousness and I'll take care of everything else."

As we conclude, I suspect there are three types of people here today. The first kind are Christians who want to serve the Lord like Elijah; who really want to obey, serve, and be involved. The message to you is to learn these lessons well—seclusion, submission, sustenance. Learn them and learn who the Lord is; spend time with Him. Maybe you're older in the Lord, and maybe in the years gone by you went through the Brook Bible Institute and God says, "Come on back for a little refresher." God uses all and any of us, and time and age are no factors with Him. You may need a refresher course. If God isn't using you the way you think you ought to be used, don't get frustrated; just learn these lessons.

But I suspect there's second group of Christians here who really aren't interested in having a unique ministry and not that interested in getting out in the public. I'm not talking about a preaching ministry or about public platform ministry; I'm talking about being out in the open and serving the

Lord and standing for Him. I think it's tragic that there might be some for whom this just doesn't matter. It doesn't even apply to them. They don't care about being trained privately because they don't care about ministering publicly. If this is you, I think you need to ask yourself if you follow the Lord God or if you follow Baal. Maybe it's not Baal; maybe it's materialism or self-interest. Whatever it is, you need to ask yourself if you really know the Lord, and if you do, then you need to commit yourself to Him. Commit yourself and let Him rule your life and you'll be a living sacrifice.

Finally, there is the third group and they are those who don't know the Lord. In fact, this message has just gone completely past them and they don't understand what I've been talking about. The main thing that you need to know is not that the Lord will sustain you financially and physically; you need to know, above all things, that the Lord will sustain you through all of eternity. That's why Jesus Christ died on the Cross—so that we would recognize that our God has and will supply the greatest need that we have, and that's for salvation—eternal salvation, the forgiveness of sins. It comes when we recognize that He is the great Supplier, and He has provided for our eternal salvation; and what is needed is simply to trust that Christ died for your sins. Repent and believe the Gospel.

These are the lessons we need to learn and take to heart as we sit in on the classes by the Brook Bible Institute. I don't know exactly where you are at in your spiritual life, but I'm certain that you fit into one of those three categories, and the Word of God demands that there be a response from you. We don't just learn the Bible for learning's sake; rather, God teaches us His Word by the Holy Spirit so that we might respond. God demands a response. If you don't know the Lord as your Savior, then I implore you to trust Him and believe on Him. Turn from yourself and put your trust in Christ as the One who died for you. If you're a Christian who doesn't want to serve the Lord, then shame on you; you've got to check out whether you really are a believer. God's word for you is to let Him teach you; humble yourself before Him and let Him break you because if you don't learn the lessons, He'll chastise you. But I trust that most of you really do want to serve the Lord, but you don't know what the Lord has for you. You just know you want to serve Him in whatever capacity you can. If so, then you've got to let Him hide you away. You've got to learn to submit even when it hurts, even when it doesn't make sense to you, even when it might seem absurd. You've got to learn that the Lord supplies your needs and He'll take care of you. Learn to look to God and you'll be ready for the ministry that God wants for you; a very fruitful ministry as He deepens your relationship with Him so you might know that the Lord God of Israel and Elijah—the Lord God of the church—lives today.

Father, we pray You will take these very practical truths and enrich our lives; and more than just enriching us, help us to respond in obedience. Help us to learn from the Lord; help us to allow You to have Your perfect way in our lives, and not to fight you but to allow You to work in our lives. We may not have a ministry of calling down fire nor have a ministry of speaking to hundreds of false prophets, but You have a unique ministry for each one of us in the body of Christ. Help us to learn these private lessons well that we might carry on in the fullness of the Spirit of God and have an effective public ministry. For this we pray in Christ's name, Amen.

---

[1] Wiersbe, Warren. *Living with the Giants: The Lives of Great Men of the Faith.* Grand Rapids: Baker Book House, 1993. 43.

[2]Harry Ironside was a wonderful man of God who served as the pastor of Moody Memorial Church in Chicago from 1930 to 1948.

[3]Hendricks, Howard. *Stories for the Heart*, compiled by Alice Gray. Portland: Multnomah Press, 1996. 272.

Chapter 2

A JEWISH QUEEN IN A PAGAN PALACE

Esther: A Study in God's Preservation of Israel
January 19, 1986

The basketball court is not the usual place that a person learns something about theology, but it was on a basketball court a number of years ago that I learned a very important theological lesson. It was there that I first realized that Christians use words which are inconsistent with biblically sound theology.

A number of years ago, I was playing a game of one-on-one basketball with a Christian friend, and I sank an incredible shot. It was truly amazing. Do you know what he yelled out? "What luck!" Now I was a fairly new Christian at the time, but it dawned on me at that moment that if God is sovereign and He controls everything, then there is really no such thing as luck. There is no such thing as chance, coincidence, accident, fate, or good and bad fortune. Things don't just happen by chance, and Christians ought to know better than to use the clichés that the world has invented to interpret the way events turn out.

You can tell the way non-Christians interpret the events of life just by the expressions they use. For instance, we hear statements such as "I guess I'm just lucky," "Those things happen, you know," "As fate would have it," "I just happened to be walking by," "I was just very fortunate," "What a coincidence," and on and on it goes. There are others such as "That's the way the ball bounces." Or perhaps you grew up hearing the expression put this way—"That's the way the mop flops," or "That's the way the cookie crumbles."

Different parts of the country have their different clichés in order to interpret life, but those expressions and clichés are unacceptable for a Christian. We shouldn't use words or expressions like that. We know that there is a sovereign God who rules over the course of human affairs in order to accomplish His divine purposes. Not only does the truth of God's sovereignty run throughout the pages of Scripture, but God specifically designated one book in the Bible to convey that message of His sovereignty. That one book is the Old Testament book of Esther.

Esther is found between Nehemiah and Job in your Bible, and it is perhaps the most unique book in the entire Bible. Why do I say that? Because it doesn't mention God's name once! It does mention a pagan king 198 times, but never is there any mention of the name of God. Also, it is never referred to in the New Testament. No New Testament writer quotes from the book of Esther. It is only one of two Bible books named after a woman—the book of Ruth being the other one. It is a book that has bothered not only unsaved Jewish scholars, but also Christian scholars.

At first glance, it appears to be only a delightful story of a young Jewish girl named Esther who is living in Persia and who was chosen to be the queen. Esther has a cousin named Mordecai who raised her, and one day Mordecai overhears a plot to kill the king of Persia. He reports this plot, but no one in the palace rewards his loyalty. In the meantime, Mordecai incurs the wrath of a Persian leader by the name of Haman. Mordecai refuses to bow down to Haman, and out of spiteful revenge and hatred, Haman determines to destroy not only Mordecai, but Mordecai's people, the Jews. Not just a few or some of them, but all of the Jews. He determines to exterminate everyone who is a Jew.

But one night something interesting happens. The king can't sleep, so he sends for a book that contains the official records of the kingdom. If you've ever been in a leadership position in a church or any other kind of leadership position, you know that the books of the official minutes would put anybody to sleep. Generally speaking, they are boring. That is what the king did. He said, "Give me the record books. I can't sleep, and I want to read what's been happening, and that will help me to fall asleep."

While reading this book, however, he comes across a record of how a plot to assassinate him was foiled, so he asks if the man who reported this plot was ever rewarded. The answer was, "No, he's been overlooked," so the king decides to reward Mordecai. In the process of rewarding Mordecai, guess who has to honor him? Haman has to honor Mordecai, a man he despises. In the meantime, Haman's plot to exterminate Mordecai and the Jews is exposed, and he is hanged on the very same gallows which he had prepared on which to hang Mordecai. The king then orders a decree which saves the Jewish people from being totally exterminated.

That is basically the story of the book of Esther in capsule form, but the Bible doesn't present a story to us just for the sake of a good story. Never think that the Bible would just present stories like any other literature book. It doesn't! There is always a message involved in the story. There is always something more than just a story. It is a sermon within a narrative. It is always a divine message, never just a story.

What is the message of Esther? The message of Esther is the providence of God. That is the key term in regard to the book of Esther—the providence of God. The purpose and theme of Esther is to demonstrate the providential care of God over His chosen people Israel.

Now what do we mean by the term "providence"? This word comes from the Latin word *providentia,* which originates from two words: *pro-* meaning "ahead" or "before," and *videre* meaning "to see." Thus, it means "to see ahead." "Foresight" would be the term we would use today—to see something before it actually happens. But with God, He not only sees what will happen, but He takes action in relation to what He sees. That is the thought of providence. It is God, who sees ahead and takes action in relation to what He sees coming ahead. Someone had defined providence as "the hand of God in the glove of history."

God is ruling the universe through providence. God is behind the scenes, shifting and directing and sovereignly manipulating the ordinary events of life to bring about His predetermined plan. Please understand that God controls the universe through providence. God only infrequently intervenes in history by means of miracles, even in the biblical record. We tend to think that miracles happened throughout the Old Testament. They didn't. Or we may think that miracles happened throughout the New Testament. They didn't. There are times in history where God breaks in and does something which we would term "miraculous." Those are events which go beyond the course of natural laws, but that's not the way God normally controls history. He takes the very ordinary, mundane, non-miraculous events that take place in the on-going of human affairs to bring about, by natural processes, those results which are divinely predetermined. In other words, it is "the hand of God in the glove of history." He is behind the scenes, bringing things to fruition in accordance with His own predetermined plan. The book of Esther was written to teach us about God's providence in preserving His people, Israel. God looked ahead in history, and He saw all the events. He saw Haman's anti-Semitic hatred, and He worked behind the scenes in order to fit those events into His divine plan, and His plan was to preserve the Jewish people.

Psalm 121:4 contains the key phrase to understand the book of Esther. It says, *"Behold, He who keeps Israel will neither slumber nor sleep."* In other words, God's back is never turned towards Israel in the sense that He is unaware of what is going on. God will always keep Israel. There is no enemy that could come in and completely destroy Israel because God is taking a nap or sleeping. He keeps Israel, and He will go on keeping Israel.

Now let me ask you a question. Would God keep Israel if they were disobedient and rebellious to Him? Would God keep Israel if they turned their backs on Him and were unfaithful to Him? A great many Christian scholars today say God would not keep Israel, that God would abandon Israel. They say that is exactly what God has done and that He is now only interested in the church. They say God is no longer interested in the Jewish people and that He is building His church and that is all He is going to build.

What does the Word of God teach? First, we need to understand that Israel was God's covenant people in the Old Testament. She was uniquely in the place of spiritual blessing and privilege. No other people, no other nation has ever been like Israel nor will ever be like Israel. Her greatest Son was the Messiah, the Lord Jesus Christ, and when He came, many Jews of the first century embraced Him and received Him. It is estimated that there were about 100,000 Jews in the first century who accepted Jesus as the Messiah, but as a nation, they officially rejected Him. No matter how many individual Jews accepted Him, as a nation, the Jews said, "No, we'll not have this Man to reign over us." But did God reject Israel? Did He say, "Away with you. I'll never have anything to do with you again"? Did God abandon her?

No! Israel temporarily has been set aside, not abandoned, not forsaken, but she has been nationally set aside.

At the day of Pentecost, God began building something new, which was never spoken of in the Old Testament. He took Jews and Gentiles, and He made something brand new called "the church," a body made up of both Jews and Gentiles. Today God is not dealing with the nation of Israel in a special relationship like in Old Testament times, but He is still preserving her. He is keeping her in spite of men like Hitler and the Arab/Israeli tensions. God is preserving His ancient people. While the church now stands in that place of special relationship and blessing to the Lord, there is coming a day when the church will be raptured. She will be taken out of the world, and once again, God will begin to deal with Israel as a national entity. The temple will be rebuilt, and more Jews will return to the land of Israel. They will go back to the Old Testament economy with sacrifices and the Law being put into effect again, and God will once again begin dealing with Israel as a national entity. He has temporarily set her aside, but He has always preserved her, and the message of the book of Esther is that God will preserve and keep Israel regardless of Israel's disobedience and rebellion to Him.

Now it is my great joy to try to burst a few theological bubbles. I take great satisfaction in doing such. Through the years, many people have looked up to Esther and Mordecai. The common Christian understanding of Esther and her cousin Mordecai is that they were godly, courageous Jews, who were spiritual examples for us to emulate. Most books dealing with Esther will explain what godly examples they were and tell us that we should follow them. There are even books with titles such as *If I Perish, I Perish*. They are based on phrases taken out of the book of Esther to encourage us to follow her great example.

I would suggest to you that while Esther and Mordecai were courageous—and there is no question about the fact that they were courageous—they were not godly, they were not spiritual, and they are certainly not righteous examples for us to follow. Having said that, let me defend my position because I think the evidence demands that conclusion. I do not say such lightly. I do not say that with haste. I have thought long about this and prayed about my conclusion, and it is not only my conclusion, but it is also my conviction that these things are true.

First of all, let's examine Esther. Esther married a pagan king. She became the wife of a pagan king by the name of Xerxes. He was a zealous pagan man who was involved in false religion. Now some say, "But she was forced against her will to do that. She had no choice in the matter." I will agree that if she was forced into the marriage, that's one thing, but if she was willful in her desire to be the queen, then it's quite another. Esther 2:8 states, *"So it came about when the command and decree of the king were heard and many young ladies were gathered to the citadel of Susa into the custody of Hegai, that Esther was taken to the king's palace into the custody of Hegai, who was in charge of the women."*

The key word is found in the phrase *"Esther was taken."* Now some say, "That means she was taken by force." It doesn't mean that at all. The Hebrew word translated *taken* does not mean forced against her will. The same word is used a few verses later in 2:15 to tell us something that she was not forced against her will to do. It says, *"Now when the turn of Esther, the daughter of Abihail the uncle of Mordecai who had taken her as his daughter…"* Mordecai *"had taken"* her as his daughter. That is the same word that is used in verse 8. I'm sure you understand the relationship of Esther and Mordecai. She was not forced against her will. She loved and obeyed this man. She was not a rebellious Jewess. She probably deeply respected her parents, and when her parents were no longer there, Mordecai took her in, and she was not forced against her will. Therefore, in verse 8, the context of the Hebrew word that is used is not saying that she was forced against her will to become the queen. She wanted to. Esther wanted to be queen of Persia, to be married to an ungodly pagan king who was involved in false religion. In fact, it was an occultic religion based on astrology.

The difference between Esther and another Old Testament woman by the name of Ruth was that Esther was a Jew married to a Gentile while Ruth was a Gentile married to a Jew. Esther was wrong. She should never have married a pagan king. Not only that, but unlike righteous Daniel, who lived around the same general time frame in history, she found no difficulty in eating non-kosher foods for many months, as seen in Esther 2:9— *"Now the young lady pleased him and found favor with him. So he quickly provided her with her cosmetics and food, gave her seven choice maids from the king's palace and transferred her and her maids to the best place in the harem."* Esther apparently had no problem eating non-kosher foods. I'm sure you recall that Daniel did. Daniel said, "I'd rather die than disobey the law of God." Daniel was a righteous Jewish man, but Esther was not a righteous Jewish woman. She had no problem whatsoever eating non-kosher foods.

She also failed to tell anyone that she was Jewish. Mordecai said to her, "Don't tell anyone. Conceal your identity," and so she did. This masquerade did not last a few days, a few weeks, or even a few months. It lasted five years. No one knew for five years, except perhaps the closest people to her. Maybe those who waited upon her knew, but basically no one else knew that she was a Jew. One scholar said, "For the masquerade to last that long, she must have done more than eat, dress and live like a Persian. She must have worshiped like one."[1] Absolutely! Logic demands that! She lived like a Persian, which meant worshiping stars and doing everything that Daniel said he wouldn't do. The more one discovers of Esther, the more it appears that her Jewishness was more a matter of birth than of religious conviction.

What about her cousin Mordecai? He was obviously an older cousin. He took her in as if he were her father, but spiritually, he was no better than Esther. Courageous, yes. Spiritual, no! He was the one who orders Esther to conceal her identity. Now someone might ask, "What was wrong with that?" The answer is that no godly Jew would have done such. God told Israel to be a light to the world and a light to the Gentiles, not to hide their identity. They were His unique people, His holy people. They were not to be violating the Law of Moses, not to be worshiping stars, not to be doing things contrary to the Law of God, yet Mordecai ordered Esther to do such. No godly Jew would have done that.

Some people say that Mordecai's godliness is evidenced by his refusal to bow down to Haman. They say, "Look! That's proof that he was a godly Jew and that he would not worship a man. He would not get into idolatry, so doesn't that prove that he was spiritual?" I don't think that is the reason Mordecai refused to bow down. Let me explain why. First of all, it was accepted custom for Israelites to fall down upon the earth before a king in an exalted position. That wasn't considered to be idolatry. 2 Samuel 14:4, 18:28, and 1 Kings 1:16 all support that. In fact, Daniel 6:21 tells us that Daniel, godly man that he was, *"spoke to the king"* – remember, he is an ungodly, pagan king – *"O, King, live forever."* Daniel was not a compromiser and he had no problem in doing that. We read basically the same thing in Nehemiah 2:3, so there was no problem in bowing down to a king. It was not idolatry.

In addition, all of the historical records indicate that Persian kings did not claim to be divine. They never claimed to be deity, so to bow down to them was not saying, "I'm worshiping you as a deity, as a god." No idolatry was involved in it.

Not only that, but later on when Mordecai replaced Haman in the exalted position in the Persian Empire, he would be expected to bow down to the king. He would have known that. I am certain he didn't have a problem doing that. It would have been understood and expected that the position called for some bowing down to the king. Do you know why I think Mordecai refused to bow down to Haman? Stubborn pride. He hated Haman, and Haman hated him. It was his stubborn, rebellious pride.

I believe that Esther and Mordecai were disobedient Jews. In fact, they were probably unregenerate, unsaved Jews. They never once speak of God. They never speak of Jerusalem, the city of David, the city of God. They never speak of the temple, the place where God was worshipped. They never speak of the Law, the reflection of God's nature. They never speak of the covenants that God made with His people. They never speak of the sacrifices, which was the only way to approach God. They never speak of prayer. They mention fasting, but never prayer, which is communion with God, or any other things that were so dear and precious to the Jewish people of that time.

In fact, Mordecai and Esther, and the majority of the Jewish people living in Persia at the time should never have been there. They were in the wrong place. They should have been back in Israel. Why do I say that? This is the time period of Ezra. Esther fits into the time frame of between Ezra 6 and Ezra 7, about the time of Nehemiah. It is when the Jews were in exile, in captivity. They went into captivity when the Babylonians stormed Israel and Judea. The Babylonians leveled Jerusalem, and they took the captives back with them. They did that at three different intervals. Daniel was one of the first to go, so the Jewish people had been in exile during the Babylonian captivity, and when the Babylonian empire lost its power, it was taken over by another group called the Medes and the Persians. That is the Persian Empire. That's where Esther and Mordecai are in the timeline of history.

It was at that time that the Jews were allowed to return to the land. In fact, Isaiah and Jeremiah said that they were commanded to return. After 70 years they were told to go back. It was captivity on a temporary basis. Jeremiah 29:10-14 says:

> *For thus says the LORD, "When seventy years have been completed for Babylon, I will visit you and fulfill My good word to you, to bring you back to this place. For I know the plans that I have for you," declares the LORD, "plans for welfare and not for calamity to give you a future and a hope. Then you will call upon Me and come and pray to Me, and I will listen to you. You will seek Me and find Me when you search for Me with all your heart. I will be found by you," declares the LORD, "and I will restore your fortunes and will gather you from all the nations and from all the places where I have driven you," declares the LORD, "and I will bring you back to the place from where I sent you into exile."'*

It was never God's intention that they stay away, not after the seventy years.

Isaiah 48:20 and Jeremiah 50:8 and 51:6 all say the same thing. "You are to go back to the land. You are not to stay in Persia. You are not to stay in Babylon. You are not to stay in captivity and in exile. Go back to the land." Why? Because God's program for the nation was centered in that land with its sacrificial system, with its temple. When the Jewish people were out of the land, they were not blessed. When the Jewish people were in the land, they were blessed. They were in the unique, specially privileged place God intended them to be when they were in the land.

People like Esther and Mordecai and the rest of the Jewish people who stayed should not have stayed. Many had gone back, but most stayed, and those who stayed applauded those who returned, and they said, "Isn't it wonderful that they've gone back to Jerusalem to rebuild the cities of Judah and the temple at Jerusalem? But we're not going to go." Why wouldn't they go? "Well, we love it here. It's convenient here. We're treated well here. We've got plenty in Persia. Why would we want to go back in a pioneering ministry? Why should we return to the leanness of Judea and Judah and Jerusalem when we've got plenty here in Persia? We're well taken care of here." And so they stayed away from Jerusalem, Israel, and Judea, yet that was the place of unique blessing and privilege.

Do you want to know how the Jewish people who were obedient people felt about it? It's recorded for us in Psalm 137. It's one of my favorite psalms. I never read it but that I can sense the absolute anguish of the people of Israel with being in captivity. This should have been the attitude of Esther and Mordecai and the other Jews. But after a period of time, they got so satisfied and so fat in the land, they just loved it there. But they should have felt like the psalmist in Psalm 137, who wrote:

> *By the rivers of Babylon, there we sat down and wept, when we remembered Zion. Upon the willows in the midst of it we hung our harps. For there our captors demanded of us songs, and our tormentors mirth, saying, "Sing us one of the songs of Zion." How can we sing the LORD'S song in a foreign land? If I forget you, O Jerusalem, may my right hand forget her skill. May my tongue cling to the roof of my mouth if I do not remember you, if I do not exalt Jerusalem above my chief joy* (vv. 1-6).

According to that, Esther and Mordecai should have had their right hands forget their skills and their tongues should have stuck to the roofs of their mouths. That's how they should have felt. That should have been their attitude. Anything to go back to Israel!

But they didn't go back. They stayed, and they were very content to stay in Persia even though God said, "Get up and get out." They had grown comfortable, and their burden wasn't for God's program to continue in the land of Israel. It is not just that they had no concern to get back in a pioneering work; they were not concerned for the program of God. To reject Jerusalem with its temple and its sacrificial system, and the Law being in effect was, in essence, to turn their backs on God. It was to say, "We're not interested in the divine program continuing. We like it this way. Thank you, Lord, but no thanks. We're very content."

What I'm saying is that Esther and Mordecai and the other Jews in Persia no longer identified themselves with God's program for Israel. They refused to identify themselves with God's program for Israel, and that's the reason God's name is not mentioned once in this book. God would not identify His name and attach it to those Jews who refused to identify themselves with His revealed program for Israel. That is so important, let me repeat it again. God's name is not mentioned at all in this book because God refuses to identify Himself and attach His name with those Jews who refused to identify themselves with His revealed program. But, in His providence, He will watch over them, and in keeping with His faithfulness and His promises to Israel, He will not abandon them. He will protect them, even if He won't identify with them. Even if He won't attach His name to them, He will preserve them.

I would like you to see this in Scripture—that God promises never to abandon Israel but always to preserve her. In Jeremiah 31:35-37 the prophet writes,

Thus says the LORD, *Who gives the sun for light by day and the fixed order of the moon and the stars for light by night, Who stirs up the sea so that its waves roar; the* LORD *of hosts is His name: "If this fixed order departs from before Me," declares the* LORD, *"Then the offspring of Israel also will cease from being a nation before Me forever." Thus says the* LORD, *"If the heavens above can be measured and the foundations of the earth searched out below, then I will also cast off all the offspring of Israel for all that they have done," declares the* LORD.

God says, "If the sun never shines again, then Israel will cease from being a nation before Me forever." If you could ever measure the heavens, then you can say that God will cast away Israel. If the stars, the moon, and the sun cease to exist, then God will cast off Israel. What God is saying is that He will never abandon His people.

Leviticus 26:27-33 is an important, but very neglected passage on this subject. God is telling Israel "if you obey Me, I'll bless you and do this and that for you." And then He says,

Yet if in spite of this you do not obey Me, but act with hostility against Me, then I will act with wrathful hostility against you, and I, even I, will punish you seven times for your sins. Further, you will eat the flesh of your sons and the flesh of your daughters you will eat. I then will destroy your high places, and cut down your incense altars, and heap your remains on the remains of your idols, for My soul shall abhor you. I will lay waste your cities as well and will make your sanctuaries desolate, and I will not smell your soothing aromas. I will make the land desolate so that your enemies who settle in it will be appalled over it. You, however, I will scatter among the nations and will draw out a sword after you, as your land becomes desolate and your cities become waste.

That's a horrible picture, but don't stop there! A few verses later, in verses 44-45, look at what God says:

*Yet in spite of this, when they are in the land of their enemies, I will not reject them, nor will I so abhor them as to destroy them, breaking My covenant with them; for I am the L*ORD *their God. But I will remember for them the covenant with their ancestors, whom I brought out of the land of Egypt in the sight of the nations, that I might be their God. I am the L*ORD.

In other words, God is saying, "In spite of all that they do, I will not abandon them. In spite of the horrible way that they've treated Me, I will not forget them." He is faithful even when they are unfaithful. If you don't understand that, then you will not understand the book of Esther. There are a lot of people who have come to the book of Esther and have turned this book into absolute nonsense. They have made it into an allegory. They have looked at the book and said, "Well, it's really about the church, and we've got see the spiritual truth here," and when they do that, they have missed the point. I don't say that arrogantly, sitting in judgment upon them, but that is missing the point of the book of Esther.

Martin Luther looked at this book and he observed, like many others have, that it mentions a Persian king about 200 times in 167 verses, and doesn't mention God once, and here's what Martin Luther supposedly concluded, "I am so great an enemy to the second book of Maccabees and to Esther that I wish they had not come to us at all, for they have too many heathen unnaturalities."[2] Luther missed the message completely, but you don't need to. The message is this—God is faithful to His Word. God keeps His promises. He will preserve Israel even if they are unfaithful. Even if they turn their backs on Him, He will preserve His ancient people.

Why is this important for us as twentieth century Christians to understand the book of Esther? There are two reasons. First, we need to understand Esther so that we understand the faithfulness of God toward us today. If God doesn't keep His word to Israel, then what assurance do we have that He will keep His word to us? If God couldn't keep His word to His ancient people, then what guarantee do we have that He will keep His word to His New Testament people?

Those of us who attended the Friends of Israel banquet yesterday were reminded that if you want to understand God's attributes, then look at the way He deals with Israel. If you want to know how holy God is, then see His holy dealings with Israel. If you want to understand God's faithfulness, then see God's faithful dealings with Israel. If you want to understand God's mercy and grace, then see how He has dealt mercifully and graciously with Israel. If you want to understand the very nature and heart of God, then understand by the way He deals with Israel. You will not understand the exact program for the church, but you will understand the attributes of God which He still exhibits in dealing with the church. Specifically, you will understand God's faithfulness. God keeps His Word.

Secondly, we need to understand what God is doing in Israel today. You may ask, "How does this book tell us what God is doing in Israel today?" I believe there is a great parallel between the Jews of Esther's time and the Jews of today. The nation of Israel today consists of many Mordecais and many courageous, zealous Jews. Many Jews around the world don't even live in the land, yet they would lay down their life for Israel.

I have a cousin who is like an uncle to me. He is my Dad's cousin. In one weekend he can, and has, raised over a million dollars for the state of Israel. There are many like him all around our nation who would do anything for Israel. No sacrifice is too great. He has no problem going up to someone and saying, "Look, you have enough money. Give a $100,000 to the state of Israel. They need it. How much can I sign you up to give?" Doing that, he has raised over a million dollars in one weekend! There are many such courageous, zealous Jews who would lay down their lives for the nation of Israel, but they are unregenerate. They don't know the Lord Jesus. They have rejected Him, and yet, in the providence of God, He has preserved that tiny nation, which by all reasonable calculation should have been wiped off the face of the earth back in 1948. There is no human explanation for Israel being in existence. None! And yet God has preserved them.

That is the same message as is found in the book of Esther. If you want to understand what God is doing in Israel today, look at the book of Esther. God is preserving His people. He is preserving them in order to be faithful to His prophetic word. Bible prophecy centers around that tiny nation of Israel. It must be in existence when the Messiah comes, because the Messiah comes to deliver Israel. The Redeemer shall come out of Zion, and He will deliver His people. There must be a literal Israel for a literal second coming of the Messiah, the Lord Jesus Christ. We understand that in spite of the Middle East tension, the Soviet oppression, Hitler in the 1930s and 40s, that *"He who keeps Israel will neither slumber nor sleep"* (Psalm 121:4). That is very important! We understand the faithfulness of God through Esther. We understand what God is doing in Israel today.

Thirdly, we understand that God's hand is involved in every area of life. There is one thing that Esther teaches that applies to us today, and that is that there are no accidents to life. Without violating man's will and without interrupting the ordinary ongoing of human affairs, God moves behind the scenes to bring about the good pleasure of His will. That is the message. That is what we have to see.

What it means is that God is in control of your life. You don't need to worry. You don't need to fear. You don't need to wonder what's going to happen tomorrow. That is what makes the Christian life so exciting and thrilling. He is leading, and He is directing through the ordinary events to accomplish His sovereign plan. It is not the miraculous that is so exciting. It is that God takes the mundane affairs of life and works it all out to bring His plan into operation. That is what is exciting. The miraculous comes and is quickly gone. The exciting thing is that God doesn't need to use the miraculous, and yet He brings about what He wants to bring about anyway.

It has been many years since I sank that basket on the basketball court and realized that there is no such thing as luck. I want you to know that on occasion I still make incredible shots, but just on occasion. There are still people who yell out, "What luck!" or "Isn't he lucky!" The difference is that now I know how to respond to them, and I do. I respond to them by saying, "Just call it sovereign luck."

That is the way we live our lives, and that is what Esther has to say to us today. God is sovereign. There are no events you need to fear. God is using everything. He is not sleeping. He is not resting. God has not taken Himself out of your life. You say, "My life is so boring to me. It's just not exciting." Listen, God is using the boring things to bring about His plan. There are a lot of people who want the excitement and the thrill and the miraculous and all of that. The exciting thing is that God doesn't need that. He is using my mundane life, and your mundane life to accomplish His will.

When I study the book of Esther, I don't get excited about Esther. I don't get excited about Mordecai. I wish they were different. What I get excited about is that here is a God—our God—who even uses man's sin to accomplish the good pleasure of His will. That is what makes life thrilling. We don't know what is going to happen tomorrow, but we know that God controls our tomorrows. He controls our enemies and the people who hate us, and He controls the people who love us. Yet He won't violate their will, but He will make sure that His will is what is accomplished in the end.

As we conclude, I trust that in the bursting of some theological bubbles, you've had your spiritual eyes expanded and broadened, and your spiritual vision has taken on new dimensions. This is just the beginning of the book of Esther, and it is exciting. God is in control. God is ruling the universe. It is the hand of God in the glove of history, and God's hand is in the glove of history in your life. I don't know what you are going through, but I want you to know that God is involved. God is going to use all things to work for His glory. We know Romans 8:28 which says that *"God causes all things to work together for good."* One of the reasons we know that is because we now understand the book of Esther.

Would you take the time to just thank the Lord that He is that kind of a God and that He is sovereign even when things look dark and bleak as they did to Esther and to Mordecai? We know by faith that God is sovereignly in charge. You don't need to be afraid of international terrorism. You don't need to be afraid of communism. You don't need to be afraid if we going to war with some other nation. You need to be interested in that kind of thing, but not afraid, because the hand of God is in the glove of history. He will preserve His people. He will build His church. He will bring about the good pleasure of His will. Thank Him for that and live in the light of that truth.

> *Father, thank You for our study tonight. Thank you that it's so helpful to see Your word so practical it affects where we are, for You're the same yesterday, today and forever. You change not. You're still preserving Israel and You're still faithful to Your church. Lord, I pray that not only will these truths be heard but that they'll be received., that You'll help us to live in the light of what we've heard tonight, to live with a new confidence in You, to live with a new understanding and a deeper understanding of Your providence, and to live with a great joy because You're in control. Help us, Lord, not to just be academic students of the Word but may what has been said tonight penetrate our hearts and effect our lives for Your glory. In the name of the Lord Jesus Christ, Amen.*

---

[1] Carl A. Baker, *An Investigation of the Spirituality of Esther*, M.Div. thesis, Grace Theological Seminary. 1977, 21-22.

[2] Martin Luther, *Table Talk*. Fount Classics Series, HarperCollins Publisher: London, XXIV, 1995, 14.

Chapter 3

How To Have God's Peace
Philippians 4:4-9
August 20, 1989

Philippians 4 explains how to have victory over worry. Most Christians struggle with the sin of worry and it may be surprising to know that even the best of apostles, at times, struggled with worry. The apostle Peter himself, from the data we can gather from the New Testament, was a worrier. How would one come to this conclusion? When the apostles recognized that Jesus was walking on the water, it was Peter who said, *"Lord, if it is You, command me to come to You on the water"* (Matthew 14:28). And Peter did. He was walking on the water until he started worrying about drowning. It is understandable why one might think like that, but he was walking on water until he started thinking about it and the possibilities of drowning.

It was also Peter, in Matthew 19, that had the following paraphrased conversation with Jesus. Peter asked, "Lord, we've given up everything for you. What will there be for us?" Jesus answered, "In the regeneration (meaning the millennial kingdom), you will sit on thrones with Me judging the twelve tribes of Israel." But there was Peter, concerned about giving up everything. "We've given up homes and possessions, all that for you. What's in it for us?" There was a worry there.

Peter worried about our Lord's statements concerning the Cross and told Him not to go to the Cross. He worried on the night that Jesus explained to them that He was leaving. He worried and made some outlandish statements concerning that. Knowing that Peter struggled with the sin of worry ought to encourage us. He learned how to have victory over that sin. That's the encouragement because it was Peter who wrote years later, *"Casting all your anxiety upon Him, because He cares for you"* (1 Peter 5:7). If Peter could learn to have victory over worry, then you and I can learn to have victory over worry. Peter was just like us. The same grace given to him, and the same Holy Spirit given to him, is given to us as well.

The way we learn about how to have victory over worry is by looking at some of the details in God's Word. Philippians 4:4-9 helps us because in this passage Paul tells the Philippians that in spite of the pressure of life, they can have victory over worry. They had pressure from persecution as well as personality clashes in the church. Remember the two women in chapter 4, Euodia and Syntyche, who were at odds with one another? They had been leaders in the church.

This church also had disunity problems. In chapter 2 he speaks about the mind of Christ and esteeming others more important than one's self. They had theological error, which is shown in the expression *"beware of the dogs"* in chapter 3. That is a term meaning "false teachers" or those who would teach error.

And so, putting it all together, Paul is saying that in spite of the pressures that you are going through as a church, and possibly as individuals, here's how you have peace in your life. Here's how you handle the pressures of life—by learning to respond in a biblical way. We can look at the ways Paul teaches us to respond to the pressures of life. Do this and I'll guarantee that you will have victory over worry. You will be obedient in this area.

First of all, respond to the pressures of life by rejoicing. He says, *"Rejoice in the Lord always. Again, I will say, 'Rejoice"* (Philippians 4:4). I think he says it twice for emphasis, and also because it's such an incredible statement that if he didn't say it twice, we might wonder about it. We may question, "Paul, is this really what you mean? You mean I can rejoice all the time? I can rejoice always?" And Paul would say, "Yes, but not because of your rotten circumstances, but in the Lord." We don't rejoice because we have cancer. We don't rejoice because we have lost our jobs. We rejoice because we're in the Lord. We understand that God is sovereign and though everything may be taken away from us, our relationship with Christ will never be taken from us. It is a joy that stems not from the fluctuating circumstances of life; those are what rob us of joy. Rather it is joy that stems from knowing that no matter what, we are in a secure relationship with Christ. That's where your mind has to go and that's where it has to dwell. We are in the Lord. So you focus on what it means to be in Christ and all that you have in Jesus Christ. Do not focus on the things that might happen to you or on the things that are being taken from you, nor on the things that are threatening your peace, but focus on what you do have in Christ. So we respond to the pressures of life by rejoicing. That is your homework assignment—to discipline your mind to rejoice.

Secondly, we respond to the pressures of life by yielding to others. *"Let your gentle spirit be known to all men"* (Philippians 4:5). That means not insisting on your own ways. Make sure that you don't insist on your rights. You will never have peace. You will be a fighting warrior kind of a person. Everyone will offend you. Everyone will be at odds with you. You will be at odds with everyone else. Life is a battle. Unless it's written in the Word of God, there are certain things that it's all right to compromise on. It's okay to not get our way. Even if people take advantage of you, it's okay because Paul said at the end of verse 5, *"the Lord is near."* And I take it that from the context that he means that the Lord's coming is close. Think about the fact that Jesus is coming back. All of our conflicts with people are so petty and trivial, and when Jesus returns, He'll give you whatever anyone took from you, and so much more. All that you feel like you lost in this life because you've lost the conflict, the Lord will reward you. He'll take care of that. It's okay. You'll get it all back, and much more.

So we respond to the pressure of life by number one, rejoicing; number two, yielding. Number three is by trusting God. Philippians 4:6 says, *"Be anxious for nothing, but in everything by prayer and supplication with thanksgiving let your requests be made known to God."* And here's the result in verse 7: *"the peace of God which surpasses all comprehension will guard your hearts and your minds in Christ Jesus."* He is saying, "Don't worry about anything." That means don't worry about a single thing. But pray about everything, even the smallest details of life. God is not waiting for us to dump the big things on Him. Life is usually made up of small, mundane things. That's what life is about. There are very few big things in life. So he says that we're not to worry about anything but to pray about everything. Cast all your care upon the Lord. God is sovereign and we trust Him. He's kind and you can give Him your problems. He's a loving Father who desires to and will take care of His children. This is more than speaking to Him. This is more than praying; it's trusting. It's meaning what you're praying, and the result will be that His peace will watch over your feelings and your thoughts so that anxiety will not arise from your mind.

So what we've looked at are three ways to respond to the pressures of life—rejoicing, yielding, and trusting. The fourth way to respond to the pressures of life if you want to have victory over worry is by meditating on the truth. Verse 8 says, *"Finally, brethren"*... and he means here not that he's moving on to a new subject but, "it only makes sense, brethren," "in light of all this, brethren, do this." *"Finally, brethren, whatever is true, whatever is honorable, whatever is right, whatever is pure, whatever is lovely, whatever is of good repute, if there is any excellence and if anything worthy of praise, dwell on these things"* (Philippians 4:8). Now this is very interesting! In verse 6, Paul tells us of what we must rid our minds. He says, "Don't worry about anything. Rid your mind of anxious thoughts. Here's what not to think about." Now in verse 8, he tells us what we have to think about, and that's very important because you and I must think about something. We don't believe that meditation is like Eastern mysticism; simply going into a corner of the room and just emptying your mind and thinking about nothing. That is not biblical meditation nor is it biblical thinking. People who worry think about the wrong things. They get into a habit of dwelling on things that cause them concern and they fret over them. They become obsessed with them. They are controlled by them. That's what Paul says we are not to think about, but we are to think about the things that are right. The battle is won or lost here in the mind concerning worry. The mind is the issue. What you choose to think about will determine whether you worry or not. Your mind matters. *"As a man thinks in his heart"* — and that's simply a synonym for the mind in this verse — *"so is he"* (Proverbs 23:7). The Bible says what you think about determines what you are. Wrong thinking leads to wrong feelings, which lead to worry and anxiety. Instead, we are to have a transformed mind. *"And do not be conformed to this world, but be transformed by the renewing of your mind"* (Romans 12:2).

Let's take this a step further. The NASB translates the Greek word *logizomai* in verse 8 as, "<u>*dwell* on *these things*</u>."

Some Bible versions say, *"think on these things."* It's actually "meditate on these things." It's not casual thought. The word means "to consider, to ponder, to meditate on, to have your mind dwell on." In fact, our English word "logical" comes from this Greek word. So the idea here is that we are to think something through logically and carefully. This is not casual thought. He's not talking about a glancing thought. We all have kinds of thoughts that glance around in our minds and you can't stop those things. But you can make sure that you don't dwell on those things. He's talking about meditating—meditating logically, thinking it through. The way to win over worry is to meditate on what is right. That means that you must discipline your mind. God is not going to do it for you. He'll give you the grace to do it, but you have to focus on what God says rather than what you have been in a habit of thinking. Focus on God rather than what the media tells you to think about or what your feelings dictate. You don't have to listen to that stuff. You and I must learn to turn off the wrong things from our minds and to concentrate on the right things.

Now, what are those right things? Well, that's the list in verse eight. I'm going to emphasize the first one and then just glance at the others because it's very difficult to keep it all straight in your mind, and I think it all comes together anyway. Paul spells out what we're to think about. Now make note of this; this is important! He begins this verse by saying, *"Finally, brethren, whatever is true..."* Now this is a most important statement. Whatever is true, we're to think about it. Now what does he mean by this? The term *true* here is opposed to false. We're to think on the things that are real and genuine; not things that might be, but things that are actual. Let me give you some insight about worry. Worry is almost always based on the future, not on the present. It's what might be, what might happen.

In Matthew 6, Jesus taught about worry and it is very helpful if you can grab hold of this. When we worry, most of the time, if not all the time, we're thinking about things that might happen in the future and we spend our time and our energy dwelling on future events. Jesus addressed this in Matthew 6:34, *"So do not worry about tomorrow; for tomorrow will care for itself. Each day has enough trouble of its own."* This is Jesus' conclusion to the whole section on worry. What does Jesus mean here? Don't worry about the future. God gives grace for today's problems. When tomorrow's problems come, and they will come tomorrow, God will give grace at that time. You don't get grace today for tomorrow's problems. Don't borrow any of tomorrow's problems; they'll be here soon enough. Only God knows what problems we'll have tomorrow.

Most of the things we worry about never happen anyway. I remember hearing the story about Dr. Donald Grey Barnhouse, a wonderful Bible teacher from Philadelphia and pastor of Tenth Street Presbyterian Church. His wife was an incessant worrier. So what he did one day is came home with a blank book, and he said, "For the next six months I want you to write down in this book everything that you worry about, everything! Don't miss anything, and after six months we'll get together and look at it." And they did that. After six months they opened the book. They went over everything. Not one thing that she had written down ever happened. Do you realize the waste of time and the dishonoring to Christ to spend your energy on that? What happens when you worry about tomorrow is that you're paralyzed today. God has given you energy to accomplish the tasks before you today and you are being robbed of that energy by worrying about what might happen tomorrow. It usually doesn't happen tomorrow and you've wasted your time and lost your energy in a paralyzed today. You'll be emotionally paralyzed and you will not have the energy to carry on the tasks that God has given you.

D. Martyn Lloyd-Jones said this: "Worry has an active imagination and it can envision all sorts and kinds of possibilities." It really can. Think about what we worry about. There are financial woes. Will I have enough money for my kids to go to college? Will I have health problems? What if I get sick? What about family problems? What about job related problems? What if this person does this to me? What if this happens in my job? What if this happens with my family? It just goes on and on and on.

We're told by the apostle Paul to dwell on the things that are true, meaning the things that are factual. That's what you have to think about, not what might happen but what is reality right now. I don't think this verse necessarily means that we have to meditate all day long on Bible verses alone. We certainly are told to meditate on the Word of God, and it certainly wouldn't be wrong to do that, but I don't think that's what Paul means here. I think what he's talking about is we are to dwell on those truths that are consistent with the Word of God. Satan is a liar. Jesus calls Satan a murderer and a liar in John 8:44. He wants to corrupt your mind with his lies. Your mind is his target just as it was with Eve. That's what Paul writes in 2 Corinthians 11:3, *"But I am afraid that, as the serpent deceived Eve by his craftiness, your minds will be led astray..."* That's why false teaching is so horrible because it aims at our thinking, and if our thinking if off, our behavior will be off.

Now how did he approach Eve? First he came to Eve and he said, "Has God said this? Has He really said this?" putting doubt in her mind about the Word of God. And then he denied the Word of God. He said, "What He says isn't true. No, you will not die." Now, that was just an outright lie. First there was a casting of doubt in her mind. "Has God really said this?" She said, "Yes, that's what He said." And Satan said, "It's not true." And then he went on to his third lie. He said that "God doesn't have your best interest at heart. He knows that on the day you eat of the fruit of this tree, your eyes will be open. You'll be like God. He doesn't want you to be like Him. He's holding back something good from you."

This is exactly, in terms of principles, how Satan works in our lives. "If God really loved you, then He wouldn't keep something from you. He really doesn't care about you. He doesn't love you like He said He did. He doesn't have your best interests at heart." And so you begin to think about this, and you buy into it like Eve. She bought into that lie and she sinned. And when Satan tried this with Jesus and he said, "Since You're the Son of God, why are you so hungry? God must not care about you. Why would God leave His Son out here in the wilderness to be hungry?" Jesus didn't buy into it and He just quoted the Scripture. He went to the Word of God and that's what you have to do. When you get those wicked thoughts and you're tempted to worry and you think, "God really isn't interested in me and I may lose this or I may lose that, or this horrible thing could happen to me," understand that Satan is out to mess up your mind. You must go back to the truth of Scripture. You need to think, "God is sovereign. God loves me. God is my Father. God promises to care for me. God has never let me down" and you start praising the Lord.

That is how David in the Psalms handled his concerns. When Saul was after him, he would complain and then he would remember how great God is, and he would burst into meditation and praise for God. That's what we have to do. Think on the *"things that are true."* Whatever is true about God and His Word and is based on the truths of His Word, think and meditate on those things. Don't believe that other stuff.

Finally, he goes on to say, "*Whatever is honorable.*" It means "whatever is worthy of respect, whatever is worthy of reverence." That's the thought here. We live in a very mixed up world; a world which honors what is dishonorable and respects what is scornful. Our heroes are often the worst of people, the people who have power and fame and money but not character. We are to think on those things and those people who are honorable. They should be our models. In fact, 1Timothy 3:8 says that deacons should be men "*of dignity.*" That's the same word translated here as *honorable.* It's the opposite of being frivolous. It doesn't mean that they are sourpusses; it just means that they are dignified as opposed to frivolous. They are those who are to be noble and serious-minded and respected and dignified and honorable. Those are the types of things we are to think about.

Next he says, "*whatever is right,*" which is to say "whatever is righteous, whatever God approves of." Meditate on those issues that are consistent with God's holiness. Just because certain things are legal and allowed in our country doesn't mean they are right. You know that! So we meditate on the righteous things. Stop dwelling on the things that the world thinks are acceptable and dwell on the things that God says are righteous. I would suggest reading good books. Going back to *"what is honorable,"* especially read great biographies—missionary biographies, biographies of great men and women of God. Dwell on those kinds of things.

Then he says, "*whatever is pure,*" and here he means "moral purity." The Philippians came from a pagan background just like our culture, and Paul tells them that it may not be easy but that they shouldn't let their minds dwell on the cesspool of life. That's the stuff in our society. Be careful what you watch on television, be careful what you listen to on radio, and be careful when people are telling dirty jokes. Get away from that stuff and be careful what you read and see in magazines. Be careful what your mind takes in. Watch what you read! Watch the information to which you are exposed! Just because everybody else is doing it doesn't make it right!

"Whatever is lovely," and this word for lovely is not external beauty but internal beauty. We live in a world that praises external beauty, but Paul says that there is a beauty of character about which we are to think. That's what he means here. We're not to dwell on those things that are ugly in nature like selfishness, hatred, arrogance. Don't dwell on that kind of stuff. Dwell on the things that are lovely in character and inner beauty.

Then he says, *"whatever is of good repute"*. He means "whatever is well-spoken of." In other words, whatever is praised by God. Whatever God speaks well of, that's what you dwell on.

Now, this is not an exhaustive list. It could have gone on, because notice what he says at the end of verse 8. He adds, *"if there is anything excellent and anything worthy of praise, dwell on these things."* In other words, he is saying you can add to this list, but make sure that whatever you add is morally excellent and praiseworthy. Throughout the day, that is where my thoughts return: "Is it worthy of praise? Is it something that's morally excellent?"

Now I don't know about you but when I go over this list, I can't keep it all straight. It all just sort of blends together, but I think it comes down to this—don't let your mind be occupied with thoughts that drag you down, upset you, bring anxiety, and defeat you in your life. Instead, dwell on those things that are consistent with the Word of God. That means you have to know the Word of God well enough to know, "Is it true?" The key is to evaluate everything in light of the Word of God and to meditate on these things.

The Bible often tells us about meditation and it says it brings stability of mind. The psalmist opens the Psalms with, *"How blessed is the man who does not walk in the counsel of the wicked, nor stand in the path of sinners, nor sit in the seat of scoffers"* (1:1). He's not in a place where he's taking in all the false stuff that his world offers, but what is he taking in? *"But his delight is in the law of the Lord, and in His law he meditates day and night"* (1:2). And notice the result: *"He will be like a tree firmly planted by streams of water"* (1:3).This is a stable, secure-minded individual. That's what meditating on the truth does for you. It drives you away from worry. When you worry, you're up and down, unstable in your thinking, unstable in your life. But if you want to be stable in your thinking, you dwell on the Word of God.

Psalm 119 is about God's Word. Seven times the psalmist says that he meditates on the Word of God. *"Those who love Your law have great peace,and nothing causes them to stumble"* (Psalm 119:165).If you want peace in your life, then you meditate on the Word of God. There is a wonderful classic statement in Isaiah 26:3— *"The steadfast of mind You will keep in perfect peace, because he trusts in You."* What you think about determines whether you're going to be a worrier or not. Don't focus on your problems. Don't focus on your difficulties. Form a habit of dwelling on what is true, what is virtuous, what is consistent with the Word of God. I would suggest getting an accountability partner and having a plan beforehand. You know you're going to be tempted to worry, so have a plan before the temptation comes so that when it comes you know what action to go into.

It would be foolish for a general to have no plan when he knows he's going to be attacked. So have a plan, a strategy, beforehand. When I'm tempted, this is where my mind is going to go. This is what I'm going to think about. It could be a Bible verse. It could be a virtuous thought that is consistent with the Word of God.

Remember this: You cannot keep from being exposed to the wrong thoughts. That's impossible. You can't keep from that becauseyou live in the world. But you can determine what thoughts you will dwell on. That's what you can determine. You don't have to dwell on wrong thoughts. You're going to be exposed to them; we all are. You can't get away from that, but you can determine and choose what you will think about. Paul says, "Think on the things that are true."

So, how do we respond to the pressures of life if we are to have victory over worry? Number one, we respond to life's pressures by rejoicing. Number two, by yielding. Number three, by trusting. Number four, by meditating. And, finally, number five, by obeying the Word. Verse 9: *"These things you have learned and received and heard and seen in me, practice these things, and the God of peace will be with you."* Meditating is important; in fact, it's wonderful –but it's not enough. That's a start, but that alone will not give you peace. You must put the Word of God into practice. You must obey and practice the truth, and that's what Paul is referring to in verse 9. He told the Philippians that they have heard his teaching and had seen him put into practice what he had taught them. He demonstrated the truth before them and was now asking them to practice and obey these things themselves and to apply them to their own lives.

Now, why will that keep you from worry? Why will that cure your worrying problem and bring you peace? It is very simple—because sin always causes unrest and anxiety. The person who has God's peace in the midst of pressure is the person who obeys the Lord, the person who has a clear conscience. As John H. Sammis says in the hymn he wrote in 1887, *"Trust and obey, for there's no other way to be happy"*—we could say 'to be joyful'—*"in Jesus but to trust and obey."* God's peace rules our hearts when we obey what we know the Word of God says. A miserable Christian is a disobedient Christian; guilt-ridden, under conviction, unhappy. That's why many Christians lack joy; they're just disobedient. That's why Paul says at the end of verse 9, *"Practice these things and the God of peace will be with you."* God who has given you peace in the sense of salvation, will then give you His peace in the sense of a calm and tranquil spirit and heart.

So what is Paul teaching us? First of all, he's teaching us that we are to rejoice. Don't fight circumstances. Rejoice in the Lord; He's sovereign and you're secure. Secondly, yield. Don't fight people. Yield to the Lord. He's coming back and He'll take care of it all. It's okay if you lose an argument. Thirdly, trust God. Don't try to fight for yourself. Don't worry about these things but trust God. Your Father cares about you. Fourthly, meditate. Don't listen to Satan. He's out to disrupt your thinking with lies. Think on the truth. And finally, obey! Don't fight God. Obey Him. Do what He says. You do that, and you'll have His peace. Let's bow together in prayer...

> *Lord, we thank You that Your Word tells us how we can have victory over worry. It's such an insidious sin. It can so destroy our effectiveness. Lord, I pray for each broth, each sister here who might be struggling with worry and it might be a way of life. I pray that they'll take these truths to heart, put them into practice, and honor You and glorify You and, like Peter someday, and say, "I used to be a worrier but now I've learned to cast all of my cares upon You. I know You care for me."*

> *Lord, I pray You'll protect our minds. I pray that You'll help us to think on the things that are true. How right Lloyd-Jones was when he said that our minds have such an incredible imagination that we can imagine all the worst things taking place; things that might happen, but they usually don't. And even if they do, Lord, we know that You'll give us grace at that time, not now. So I pray that You'll help us to be a people who are free, free in our hearts, free*

in our minds. The Son has set us free. I pray that You'll make that so precious to us that our meditation would be on this glorious truth. We pray this in Jesus' name, Amen.

Chapter 4

THE SPIRITUAL MARATHON
Hebrews 12:1-3
February 14, 1993

In 490 BC a battle took place near the small Greek town of Marathon. The invading Persian army was caught by surprise by the outmanned Athenians who charged into their ranks and saved the Greek Empire. Legend has it that a Greek soldier by the name of Pheidippideswas ordered to run to Athens and tell them the news of this great victory. His run of about 26 miles from the battle field to Athens is considered to be the first marathon run. Unfortunately for Pheidippides he wasn't as fit as many marathoners are today, because when he entered Athens and proclaimed, "Rejoice! We conquer!" he collapsed and died.

I don't know if that story is historically accurate. I don't think anyone knows. It may be, but we don't know for certain. But I do know that running a marathon race is hard. This last year, I trained and ran in the New York City marathon on November 1st. You may never attempt anything as silly as that, but the Bible teaches that the Christian life is like a marathon race. Where does the Bible teach that? Hebrews 12:1-3. The writer says,

> *Therefore, since we have so great a cloud of witnesses surrounding us, let us also lay aside every encumbrance and the sin which so easily entangles us, and let us run with endurance the race that is set before us, fixing our eyes on Jesus, the author and perfecter of faith, who for the joy set before Him endured the cross, despising the shame, and has sat down at the right hand of the throne of God. For consider Him who has endured such hostility by sinners against Himself, so that you will not grow weary and lose heart.*

Please notice a few things that will help put this portion of Scripture into perspective. First, in a number of places the Bible compares the Christian life to a foot race; not only a marathon, but also a foot race. One place is 1 Corinthians 9:24-27. Paul writes:

> *Do you not know that those who run in a race all run, but only one receives the prize? Run in such a way that you may win. Everyone who competes in the games exercises self-control in all things. They then do it to receive a perishable wreath, but we an imperishable. Therefore I run in such a way, as not without aim; I box in such a way, as not beating the air; but I discipline my body and make it my slave, so that, after I have preached to others, I myself will not be disqualified.*

The emphasis in this portion of Scripture is the aspect of discipline. Runners who win are disciplined. They work at it. It doesn't happen by accident. So the parallel is: Effective Christians who are used by God are disciplined. They have self-control. They are disciplined like a well-toned athlete.

Galatians 5:7 is another passage which uses this running analogy. By the way, I am convinced that if the Apostle Paul were alive today, he would read the sports page in the newspaper every day because he had such an interest in athletics. He often speaks of running and athletics and discipline, so Paul knew about the athletic games of his day. And in Galatians 5:7 he writes, *"You were running well; who hindered you from obeying the truth?"* The emphasis here is on making progress. These Galatians were running at a nice pace, making spiritual progress, and then the Judaizers—the legalists—came in and said, "Oh, salvation is not just by grace; you have to add some works to the Christian life." As a result, the Galatians were hindered in their progress. They were slowed down by legalism. That's the emphasis there.

Second Timothy 4:7 speaks of another aspect of the race. Paul says, *"I have fought the good fight, I have finished the course, I have kept the faith."* The emphasis here is on finishing the Christian life well. What he means is, "I have been obedient to the course that God set before me. I'm coming down the home stretch; I'm about to die and I have finished my life. I have run the race that God had for me."

But in Hebrews 12:1-3, there is a different emphasis. I wanted you to see these other portions of Scripture because Paul isn't just saying, "Run." When he says, "Run," in each of those passages, there is a different aspect and a different emphasis of the race in each passage. The same is true in Hebrews 12; the emphasis there is different also. Now he does mention finishing, and we'll talk about that, but that is not the overall theme and emphasis. The main thought in Hebrews 12 is endurance. In fact, the word translated *race* in verse 1 is the Greek word, *agōn*. That sounds very similar to our English word "agony," because that is the source from which we get that word. The race he is referring to is not a short sprint. It's not a hundred yard dash or a hundred meter dash. That's not the race to which he is referring, but rather, he's referring to an agonizing run. He's referring to a marathon. A run of endurance. That's why he says that the race is to be run with endurance in verse one. At the end of the verse he says, *"let us run with endurance the race that is set before us."* You really don't have to endure a hundred yard dash. It's not an endurance race. It's not easy, but it's not an endurance run. In other words, we're not to give up. That's the thought here. We're to persevere regardless of the difficulties and the trials of life under agonizing circumstances. We are to continue with a firm commitment to Jesus Christ.

Why would he say that? Because that is precisely what the Hebrews of the first century needed to hear. They were tempted to waver in their faith. Remember, some of these people were not believers. There are warning passages that are too severe for believers. But most of these people had accepted Christ. They had come out of Judaism. They had accepted Christ, but the Jewish community was putting incredible pressure on them to abandon their faith and compromise. In chapter ten, he speaks about their suffering and the persecution. Some of them were thrown in prison. Some of them were mocked and ridiculed publicly. Others had their property seized. So some of them said, "We want to quit. It's not worth it! It's too hard for us. Our families are against us. Our friends have turned against us. It's just too difficult." They were probably even outcasts from the synagogue. So he says, in 10:35, *"Therefore, do not throw away your confidence."* That is, the confidence you once had in Christ, don't throw it away. He adds, *"which has a great reward."* There is a reward. There is a future ahead. Don't throw it away now. Verse 36: *"For you have need of endurance, so that when you have done the will of God, you may receive what was promised."* You need to endure because some day the race will be over and that's when you get the reward. That's when you get the prize, so don't throw the prize away now. Don't lose heart; don't give up. That's why at the end of verse 3 he says, *"so that you will not grow weary and lose heart."* Why would he say that? Because some of them were growing weary and losing heart. So he's talking about endurance. Some of them started off well, but now they were into the fifteenth mile of a marathon and it was tough.

We need to hear the same message, because there are some people who view the Christian life as a sprint. They start well and they make great strides quickly, but then things become a little tough. Maybe they receive some ridicule, or maybe God has a certain course for them that is not easy, and they are called to suffer a little bit. So they compromise and slow down or even stop. Then they go to a weekend seminar and they get pumped up again and they sprint a little bit and then they stop again. Then they hear a message in church and they do a little sprinting that week, but then they slow down again and finally collapse and can't go on. So there are some believers who are just up and down in the Christian life because they view it as a sprint rather than seeing it as God presents it, which is that it is a marathon race. It is an endurance event. God wants us to run steadily; He wants us to endure, and He will bring us to the finish line.

The Jewish people to whom Hebrews was written were getting weary in the Christian life, just as there are times that you and I get weary in the Christian life. There are times when we feel like giving up—and I don't mean giving up in the sense of saying that we will no longer follow Jesus Christ, because no true believer would ever do that—but weary in the sense of compromise and backing off. Maybe God has called you to the mission field and you say, "No, I can't trust you for that, Lord. I've got all kinds of problems." Or perhaps God has called you to be in a tough, difficult job situation and you say, "No," and you begin to think in a secular, non-biblical manner. You get your eyes off of the Lord and you get your eyes on people and yourself, and all of a sudden, you have some serious setbacks in your Christian life and you're not making the progress that you once were. Those are the wearisome times. Those are the times when you have given up and the times where you have lost heart.

We have many missionaries here this morning, and there are times when they get discouraged, and those of you who are not missionaries need to know that. Sometimes they go through the trial of a lack of interest by fellow Christians. They are out on the field alone, and they haven't gotten a letter from home in weeks or months, and they wonder if anyone really cares. Or perhaps it is a trial of a lack of funds. Prices all over the world are rising and inflation where they are serving may be soaring. Then there is the weariness of loneliness. There's no one to whom they can really open up. They can't share with those they've been sent to minister to about their problems; after all, they are there to help them with their problems. Also, there's a lack of responsiveness on the part of those to whom they minister. They've been out there for years and there's hardly any response, or there was a response and now those believers are growing weary, and that's all a burden to the missionary. Then there are conflicts with fellow missionaries. They've been sent to proclaim God's love to the lost, but perhaps they can't even get along with another fellow missionary. There are discouragements of deputation, and conflicts with government officials and unbelievers, and disappointments over the sinful behavior of other believers, and the normal problems that we all have with our families, health, and other things going wrong. There are times when all of us—both missionaries and those of us who are not on the mission field—grow weary and tired and lose heart. Pressures and temptations seem to overwhelm us and we honestly ask ourselves is it really worth it to be sold out to Jesus Christ. And sometimes, by our actions, we say, "No, it's not." Then what? If you find yourself thinking, "Is it really worth it? I don't know," then you need to really take a careful look at Hebrews 12:1-3. In this passage the writer gives us two encouragements to keep running the race; to keep running the spiritual marathon even when we feel like quitting.

Listen: there are plenty of times when we feel like quitting. It's not wrong to feel like quitting, it's just wrong to quit. It's not wrong to feel like quitting—that's called temptation. At times all of us feel like quitting, not being as sold out, not being as zealous, just sort of lying back and saying, "Why do I have to be on the front lines? Why can't I just be in the background?" There are many times I've wondered about that—and wished for that. That's when I need to turn to Hebrews 12 and examine it closely, because in this passage, there are two encouragements to keep running the race when we feel like quitting.

Encouragement number one: Remember the Old Testament heroes of faith. Verse 1: *"Therefore, since we have so great a cloud of witnesses surrounding us, let us also lay aside every encumbrance and the sin which so easily entangles us, and let us run with endurance the race that is set before us."* The writer begins by telling us that we are surrounded by a great cloud of witness. What is this great cloud of witnesses to which he is referring? The word "therefore" connects chapter 11 with chapter 12. In chapter 11 he talks about the heroes of faith. So what he does in 12:1 is look back and he says, "Based on what I've just told you about these men and women in the Hall of Fame of faith— 'Therefore...' Here's the application. These are the ancient champions of faith who, by their faith. persevered through all sorts of trials and difficulties in earlier generations."

They ran the race. They ran their spiritual marathon and they finished. They did it. They endured. They knew how to run the race of faith. Like Noah and Abraham, they trusted God's Word when they couldn't see the fulfillment of that word. But they believed God. Like Moses, they made decisions based on faith that resulted in hardship and suffering.

Moses refused to be called the son of Pharaoh's daughter, and even though his association with the people of God would mean ill treatment, he persevered. Like Rahab, who believed in God in spite of the fact that nobody else in her society believed in Him. She dared to believe and trust that God was true to His word, and so she went against the whole of her society. The men and women of chapter 11 ran the race and they finished. This cloud of witnesses endured to the end. They knew how to run a spiritual marathon without quitting. They finished their race. So now, the writer is saying it's our turn to run. These people offer encouragement to us to race without dropping out due to weariness.

The question is, how do they offer us encouragement to run? How do they motivate us and spur us on? Let me give you a popular and rather common interpretation of this verse. Some have interpreted this verse to be saying that the Christians who have died before us are in heaven now looking down on us, watching us, as though they are in the stands of a stadium and we're on the field, and they are spurring us on, saying, "Go! Run! Finish your course!" That's a nice thought, but that's not what this verse is teaching.

Before I explain what it is teaching, let me answer a question which may be going through your mind: Do people in heaven see us? Are they aware of what's going on? My answer is that we're not told in Scripture. It is pure speculation. We don't know what they know. We don't know what they see. The Bible doesn't tell us. Anything that anyone comes up with is just their opinion. People in heaven may see what's going on, but then again, they may not. We do know from the Book of Revelation that they are gathered around the throne of the Lamb, praising Him. In my feeble way of thinking, if I was in heaven and was given the option between looking at the Lord and looking at fallen mankind, my answer would be, "I'd rather look at the Lord!" So, it's a nice thought, but that's all it is. They may, indeed, look at us, but that is not what this verse is talking about.

What is the verse saying? First of all, these people are not spectators. The writer does not say we have so great a cloud of spectators; he calls them *"a cloud of witnesses."* The word "cloud" means a large crowd or host of people. But these people are not witnessing what we're doing; that isn't his point. They are witnessing in the sense that they are testifying to us that the race of faith can be run and that God will see us through; that faith in God is worth it. They testify to us. They witness by their lives in the pages of Scripture that we can endure because they endured; they made it. God gave them grace and strength for every kind of situation, and if they can do it, we can do it, too. They speak to us even though they are dead; they speak to us through the pages of Scripture. They made it through life's heartaches by faith in God and we can too. God never let them down and He'll never let us down, because the reason they made it was because of their God—and their God is our God.

You can endure. You can endure through all the trials and difficulties of life just like the Old Testament heroes did by faith in God. These people were not super-duper saints. I don't know anyone who is a super-duper saint. They were ordinary people with failures and struggles. Rahab was a prostitute and Abraham lied. We know about Jacob and Isaac; those men were just people of clay. All of them were men and women of clay. If they could make it by faith, we can too. These Old Testament characters offer tremendous encouragement to us to press on when we feel like giving up. I'm sure they felt like giving up, and they didn't have the benefits of all the revelation that we have. The reason they encourage and inspire us is that they endured the hardships of the walk of faith before us and they proved it can be done. When I was training for the New York City Marathon, if I had asked, "Has anyone ever finished this course?" and the response was, "Nobody's ever finished; they all drop out," I probably would have done something else instead. In the Christian life, when we read about others who have gone on before us and they've made it, it gives us great encouragement, because we then know that we can make it too.

This is why you want to be familiar with the Old Testament characters. Paul tells us in Romans 15:4, *"For whatever was written in earlier times* (that's the Old Testament) *was written for our instruction, so that through perseverance and the encouragement of the Scriptures we might have hope."* So one reason the Old Testament was written was to give us hope and encouragement that others have successfully lived the life of faith in Christ.

Let me explain how this works. When you don't know what God's plan is for you or what the next step is, but you've been obedient up to that point even though you don't know what His plan for you is down the road, you may become tempted to be anxious and worried and begin to wonder, "Where am I going to end up and where will this lead?" Then Abraham witnesses to you because God called him to obey without knowing where he was going and yet he made it by faith (cf. Hebrews 11:8). He went out not knowing where he was going. God just said, "Get up and leave. Leave everything that's comfortable to you." It may be that God is calling you to do something like that. Maybe He's calling you to the mission field. Maybe He's calling some of the missionaries here today to a new field. Maybe He's calling you to take a step of faith. You don't know where He wants you, and you're tempted to say, "That's too rough, I don't want to do that." But then Abraham speaks to you and he witnesses that you can do it.

Or, God calls you to do something and you know it is going to result in problems and great hardship in your life and you wonder, "Should I do this? It might cost me my life. It might cost me economically." Then the parents of

Moses witness to you that, by faith, they did what was right. By faith, they hid Moses and God gave them the strength and grace not to fear the wrath of the Pharaoh (cf. Hebrews 11:23).

Or, God allows tremendous physical pain and mental anguish to enter your life and you wonder if you can go on trusting God throughout that illness, with its heartaches and the agony of pain. Then, countless Old Testament characters step forward and testify that God gave them the strength to endure to the end because they trusted Him. Hebrews 11:36-38 says: *"others experienced mockings and scourgings, yes, also chains and imprisonment. They were stoned, they were sawn in two, they were tempted, they were put to death with the sword; they went about in sheepskins, in goatskins, being destitute, afflicted, ill-treated (men of whom the world was not worthy), wandering in deserts and mountains and caves and holes in the ground."*

They didn't give up and you don't have to give up either. You can endure. That's how it works. Their lives spur us on and encourage us to make the right choices in life based on faith in God's Word, even when we don't have the right feeling. Feelings are not the same thing as faith. Don't worry about your feelings. Your feelings can deceive you. Even if you don't have the right feelings or you don't understand what God is doing in your life, you still run the spiritual marathon. You can trust Him to give grace and strength, even if you don't know what He's doing. You can still trust Him. Old Testament characters did, and they didn't know what was going on. How do we know we can trust Him? How do we know He'll give us grace? Because a great cloud of witness constantly speak to us by their examples of faith. They endured by faith, therefore, we can too.

But how? How do we keep running a spiritual marathon when so many things seem to get us down, discourage us, and hinder our progress? Verse one goes on to say, *"let us also lay aside every encumbrance and the sin which so easily entangles us, and let us run with endurance the race that is set before us."* That's how we do it. Let me explain. As a runner, one of the things that I've learned is to run light. You don't want extra weight on you. I'll never forget my first race. It was a four mile run called the "Race for the Pies." It was a rainy, cold January day, so I thought I would bundle up. I wore sweat pants and a sweat shirt. That's okay if you take them off at the start of the race, but I didn't do that. As we ran, the rains just came and after a while I realized that I had put on a few pounds. My sweat suit just got wetter and heavier. I must have been carrying an extra 5 or 10 pounds. Now, in the physics of running, the force of each step is equal to three times whatever your weight may be, so that was like carrying an extra 15 to 30 pounds. Consequently, I was injured in that race because the extra weight hindered me. Marathon runners—in fact, any kind of distance runners—are very conscious of running "light." They don't want any extra weight, so they wear light clothing. I recently purchased some new running shoes, and I was very conscious of the fact that my new running shoes were lighter than my old pair. They were only one ounce lighter! You may say, "That's nothing!" But when you're running 26 miles, that one ounce is something. At the New York City marathon, there was a place before they could check the runners' body fat. Runners are very concerned about those things. At the start of the race, many of us had sweatshirts on, but after we had run a few miles, we just throw that stuff off. Interestingly, the Salvation Army came along behind us and picked those sweatshirts and other garments up and gave it to the poor in New York who could use them. So you see, you want to run light. That's what the writer is saying to the Hebrews.

This preoccupation with "lightness" is what all of us should have in the Christian spiritual marathon. He says we are to *"lay aside every encumbrance."* The word *encum-*

brance means weight or burden. In ancient times it was used to refer to excess body weight. In other words, extra body fat. It could mean clothing as well. Now here is where we want to deal with the Hebrews' unique situation. What was it that was weighing down the Hebrews and hindering their faith? That's what the writer is talking about. What was it for them? It was the legalism of Old Testament Judaism that God had said had ended, yet they were still involved in it. It was their old way of life that was hindering them—the Old Testament rules, the regulations, the ceremonies, the "dos and don'ts" of Judaism with its sacrifices and temple worship and high priests. It was that to which they were tempted to retreat back. They were still trying to hold on to those things, and the message of Hebrews is simply that Christ is better. "Let go of that old stuff. Anything that you ever had in Judaism, Jesus is better, He is superior." That's the message of the book of Hebrews.

And while those things were not sin in-and-of themselves, they were unnecessary weight. Sacrifices weren't sin. Temple worship wasn't sin. The high priestly order—God had instituted that, so how could that be sin? But now they were unnecessary weights that hindered the Hebrews from running the race of faith. Those Judaistic rules became standards by which they tried to please God. They became external standards. And God said, "There is only one thing that pleases Me." Back in 11:6 He said, *"without faith it is impossible to please [God]."* These people weren't running by faith. They were running by externals. In fact, that's exactly what happened to the Galatians. They had the same problem. They were running a nice steady race and then the legalists came in and said, "You've got to do this, you've got to do that."

I'm afraid that these legalistic weights still hinder Christians today, only they are not Jewish legalistic weights, they are Christian legalistic weights. Some of us are still trying to please God by some external type of behavior and we've neglected the heart. We've neglected internal obedience and submission and genuine faith. We think that if we just perform a certain external behavior, it will make us more spiritual than others. The way we spend Sundays—those "forbidden activities" on Sundays—if you just stay away from those, you're more spiritual. And perish the thought that someone should do something that doesn't meet your approval; then you say, "They're not spiritual," even though the Word of God doesn't teach anything like that. Or there are certain types of recreation and entertainment, or how we dress. If somebody dresses a little bit differently—perhaps they wear certain jewelry that you don't approve of—we mark them as being unspiritual, and assume that we're more spiritual because we don't do that. Perhaps the issue is a certain hair style or the length of one's hair, or maybe it's whether or not someone has a beard.

A lot of Christians who think they are out in front in the Christian race are really lagging behind. They aren't spiritual, but they think they are spiritual. It's just Christian legalism. It will hinder your real walk with God and real spiritual progress, and that's the insidiousness of legalism. You think you're making progress because you've got all these externals, but you are not. You're losing. You're far behind. You're running a seven hour marathon.

If you focus on externals, when the real pressures come, you won't have any internal fortitude to deal with them, because everything is external. Everything is outward. And when some real trouble comes, you have not really trusted the Lord; you have not gotten on your knees before Him and said, "God, I don't feel anything. I don't understand what's going on, but I trust the Word of God." But if you're caught up with all these externals and you think that's spirituality, when the real pressures hit, you're not going to be able to endure.

But it's not only the extra weight of legalism that hinders our progress. It is also a specific sin that he's talking about. Notice verse 12 where he says, *"and the sin which so easily entangles us."* I believe that up until that statement the weights he refers to are not sins in-and-of themselves, but at this point he begins talking about the sin. Not just a sin in general, it's *"the sin."* What was the sin that hindered the Hebrews? It was doubt and unbelief. As you go through this book, that there are a number of times the writer speaks about unbelief and doubt; especially in chapter three. He says, *"Today if you hear His voice, do not harden your hearts, as when they provoked Me"* (3:15). That's what the warning passages are about. That's how Hebrews 6 should be interpreted (cf. Heb. 6:4-6). What it's saying—and by extension to all of us—is, if you want to run a good race, then throw off the sin of doubt or unbelief. Throw it off and take God at His Word. That's how the heroes of faith lived.

Noah resisted the temptation to say, "I've never seen rain, so it must not be true. I'm not going to build an ark. I'm not going to do it because I've never seen it." No, Noah went out by faith and took God at His word even though he didn't have clue as to what rain was. Abraham didn't say, "I've never heard of anyone being raised from the dead before." He didn't say, "God said to sacrifice Isaac, yet all the promises are wrapped up in him. No, I'm not going to do that." But the Bible says in Hebrews 11:17-19 that Abraham was about to sacrifice Isaac, believing that God would raise Isaac from the dead, even though he had never seen a resurrection. Joshua didn't say, "I don't believe God is going to bring the walls of Jericho down. What a silly thing to do! March around the walls—we'll be ridiculed, we'll be laughed at. What kind of way is that for a Jewish army to act? 'Go march around Jericho's walls.' Humph!" But he didn't say that. Why? Because he, and the rest of those men, believed God.

All of us are tempted to doubt. Ephesians 6:11-17 specifically tells us about the armor of God, and one of the things God has provided for us in the analogy between a Roman soldier and a Christian soldier is found in verse 16. He says, *"in addition to all, taking up the shield of faith with which you will be able to extinguish all the flaming arrows of the evil one."* The *"evil one"* is Satan. The shield about which he was speaking was a large shield; he's not speaking about a small shield. There are different kinds of shields, but he's speaking about a large shield that covered a Roman soldier's body. In Roman warfare, the enemy wanted to eventually engage in hand-to-hand combat with the soldier. But he had to get the soldier to drop his protective shield in order to do that, so they would fire flaming arrows or darts which had been dipped in pitch at the soldier. If the arrows missed the shield and hit the soldier, they would obviously burn him. I understand the arrows would burst into greater flames and the soldier would let down his shield, stop moving, and he would be unprotected. Then the enemy would rush in and could defeat the soldier in hand-to-hand combat. In the same way our enemy, Satan, throws flaming darts at us in the form of temptations to doubt and not believe God. If you let those darts hit you, they're going to burst into more areas of doubt and spread, and then you're going to stop moving and you'll be defeated.

What is the shield of faith? It is our trust in God's Word. It is trusting that what God has said is true; that's the shield of faith. It's obvious that God has a course laid out for us. His unique plan for your life is not His plan for my life; my plan is different. He has a unique course for every one of us, and for some, it may be to go the mission field. It may be to do something that's difficult. It may be a rough situation. We're all tempted to try to avoid running that course, because we don't believe God. That's the bottom line—we don't believe God enough to trust Him to give us the grace in those situations. So, some of us who have gotten off course have dropped out. What you need to do today is get back on course, because the Old Testament heroes of faith say to us, "We stayed on course and God was true to His Word." So we've got to get back on course. Get back in the race. It's our turn to run, and as we run, we're going be given a second encouragement to keep running even when we might feel like quitting.

The first encouragement is the Old Testament heroes of faith; the second encouragement—which, by the way, is something that the heroes of faith didn't have—is the example of Jesus Christ. Verse 2: *"fixing our eyes on Jesus, the author and perfecter of faith, who for the joy set before Him endured the cross, despising the shame, and has sat down at the right hand of the throne of God."* All good runners stay focused. They don't allow things to distract them in a race, such as other people or noise. I once watched a video of the New York City Marathon, and I recall the announcer predicting that a certain runner from South Africa was going to win even though the runner he was speaking about wasn't ahead at that point. But the announcer, a former runner himself, said, "Notice his eyes. He's not being distracted, he's looking straight ahead. But look at the other man. He's turning his head, he's looking around, and that's a sign he's growing weary; he's growing tired." That was accurate. The South African kept his eyes fixed ahead and he won, because he wasn't distracted. I, on the other hand, finished 18,748 out of 27,000. Why? Because I purposely allowed everything to get my attention. I purposely didn't stayed focused. Not that I would have challenged the guys in front even if I had stayed focused, but I would have finished better if I had. But it was my first marathon, so I took in the sights and sounds and the noise and smells of New York City. That's what I wanted to do.

That's true of sports in general. When a baseball batter steps up to bat, the coach doesn't say, "Keep your eye on the pitcher," he says, "Keep your eye on the ball; stay focused." When you're playing defense in basketball, you are to stay focused on the basketball and watch it. But in the spiritual marathon known as the Christian life, we are to stay focused on one object, and that is the Lord Jesus Christ.

Notice that verse two refers to Him as Jesus. Not Jesus Christ; not even the Lord Jesus Christ. Why? Because the writer's emphasis here is on the earthly life and ministry of our Lord and in His earthly life and ministry, He was called Jesus. The writer tells us to fix our eyes on Jesus and the way He lived on this earth. How did He live? By faith. That's why He's referred to as *"the author and the perfecter of faith."* He is the author in the sense that He is the leader of faith. In other words, He is the supreme example of how to live by faith. He is the perfecter of faith in the sense that He's complete. The word *perfect* means "to complete a goal." Hecompleted the race of faith. He finished His course with triumphant faith. He is the supreme example even beyond the Old Testament characters of how we are to run the race of faith. Jesus lived by faith like nobody else. In fact, even though while He was on earth, He was the God-man (in fact, He is the God-man even now), He didn't operate in His own strength and His own divine power. As a man, He trusted the Father. He lived in the power of the Spirit, but He lived as a man. That's why He's our supreme example. For example, His prayer life was a life of faith. His resistance to Satan demonstrated His trust in God's Word. His humble trust in the Garden of Gethsemane was a demonstration of His faith. 1 Peter 2:23 says, *"while being reviled, He did not revile in return; while suffering, He uttered no threats, but kept entrusting Himself to Him who judges righteously."* Even though He was cursed at, He didn't scream back at them. Even His last words on the cross were words of faith. He said, *"Father, into Your hands I commit My spirit"* (Luke 23:46). He always had faith. Even His enemies recognized His trust in God. As He was on the cross, they said, *"He trusts in God; let God rescue Him now"* (Matthew 27:43).

But how did Jesus endure the cross? Have you ever asked yourself that question? How did He endure the cross? Verse 2 tells us: *"who for the joy set before Him endured the cross, despising the shame, and has sat down at the right hand of the throne of God."* The reason that Jesus did not waiver or quit in the race was because of the joy awaiting Him at the finish line. There was exultation and glorification, which included the satisfaction of finishing the work He had been sent to do by bringing many sons and daughters to glory. The exultation and glorification—that's what kept Him going. He knew what was waiting for Him, because Psalm 16:11 says, *"In Your presence is fullness of joy; in Your right hand there are pleasures forever."* He knew that referred to Him because it was a messianic Psalm.

What is the writer to the Hebrews saying to us? How do we apply it our life? His point is this: When you feel like giving up and you're discouraged over your circumstances, or you've been burned by somebody and you're really having some difficulties, you need to think about Jesus and the circumstances He faced and how He endured the cross. It was the most degrading punishment, reserved only for those considered sub-human. That's what Jesus endured. And He despised the shame. He didn't say, "Oh, the cross is wonderful." No, He despised the shame. He was crucified as One who was cursed by God and disgraced by man. But Jesus persevered and endured it even though He despised the shame. That's why we need to fix our eyes on Him. Because no matter what you and I go through, it will never ever be as tough as what He went through – never. Never will it be as tough. But He didn't give up and disobey. That's why the writer says in verse 3, *"For consider Him who has endured such hostility by sinners against Himself, so that you will not grow weary and lose heart."* Whenever you think of giving up, look at Jesus, because He never gave up, and you have never gone through anything like He's gone through.

Let me tell you something which is very practical. The problem with many of us is that our eyes are fixed on people other than Jesus. In fact, the Greek word in verse two which is translated *"fixing our eyes"* literally means *"look away"* to Jesus. Turn away from whatever you're looking at. It may be other people. It may be that your eyes are fixed on a particular pastor or some well-known Bible teacher, or teachers at school or close friends. And if they fall spiritually, what happens? You are devastated. Why? Because your eyes got off of Jesus; perhaps even looking at yourself and your problems. I do not endorse the modern, so-called "Christian" counseling approach that says, "Let's look within; let's look at ourselves. Let's look at our background." I don't want to look at my background. I don't want to look within. That's depressing. I'm here for help. I don't want to be more discouraged than when I first came in. I don't want to know how I got these problems; that's not biblical. I want to know how to get rid of them. The Bible says, "Turn away from your problems, turn away from yourself, and look to Jesus."

So, get your eyes off of other people (and even yourself and your own problems) and fix your gaze on Christ and leave it there. Study the Gospels; learn what went into His perseverance and remember, what kept Him going is the same thing that needs to keep us going and that is the joy at the finish line. We have a finish line too, and there is so much joy there. That's what you need to remember. The joy of what? Being in His presence; the joy of our inheritance, and the joy of spiritual rewards. Romans 8:18 basically says, "It will be worth it all when we see Jesus." We need to run that spiritual marathon, looking forward to hearing those words at the finish line, *"Well done, good and faithful slave...enter into the joy of your master."*

Let me tell you something I've learned from my personal experience of running a marathon. It's also true in the spiritual realm, and that's why I'm bringing out these things to you. There is no joy in running a marathon apart from the first few miles. It is not fun. It's not something you just go out and say, "I think I'll have some fun today." It is pure agony. During the marathon, after the first few miles, my left knee began to throb. I had to take two extra strength pain relievers just to continue. After a while, my legs felt like lead. I felt like I was shuffling them. They weren't rising; they were just moving along. My energy was gone. I wasn't even thinking clearly. In fact, when we got into Central Park, all of the people were cheering us on and giving words of encouragement. But there was one fellow in Central Park who was yelling at us. Now, by the 22nd mile, you're not thinking clearly. I can only compare it to how a woman in labor must feel at the end of her labor. Because the thought that ran through my mind was, "I'm going to grab this guy. I'm going to pull him out and stomp on him." If I had had the energy, I think I would have done that. So I wasn't even thinking straight.

At about the 23rd mile, I heard voices in my head. I heard my family saying, "Finish! Don't come back unless you finish!" Words like that—finish! I would have crawled to the end if I had to. I didn't go fast enough to hit what's called "the wall," but many people hit the wall somewhere between the 18th and the 21st mile. Your body switches over to another energy level or a different fuel from your body. It's a horrible feeling. I've hit the wall in other runs, but not that day. But it is not fun.

So what, then, would compel someone to do something like run a marathon? Do you know why you continue? For the same reason we are not to quit the Christian race. The joy at the finish line. That's all you think about. "This will be over. This will be over soon." There's joy at the finish line. There is nothing quite like the feeling of crossing the finish line to the cheering throngs of the people in Central Park and then you receive a medal!

I want to close by reading about the finish line. It's a book by Knute Larson called *Run Steady, Run Straight.* He writes about one marathon runner's description of what it's like to run in a marathon and then he compares it to the Christian life. Here's what this marathon runner said.

> The start of the marathon is joyous. After all those weeks of training, and anticipation, and anxiety, the physical release of beginning the race is a pure high. Like children rushing out for recess, we're finally moving. Some children in the yard up ahead are holding up a hand lettered sign that says, 'Baskin Robbins one mile'. I wonder what would happen if all the would-be marathoners decided to forget the whole thing and just go eat ice cream. Would it spoil some vast eternal plan? Maybe it would. Ten miles and all's well. Try not to subtract ten miles from 26 if you can help it. The runners aren't talking and laughing now, everyone seems to be absorbed in his own personal struggle.
>
> Twenty-one miles. Yes, Virginia, there is a wall. It's alive and well and living in Michigan and it just keeps falling on me. Not one big crash just a whole bunch of little ones. The ceilings and floors are crumbling, too. The whole building has been condemned. Can a condemned building run five more miles? There are a lot of people walking up ahead. Does the universe care if you stop and walk in a marathon? Do I care? If I stop and walk, will the earth stop revolving around the sun or something?

Four more miles. Or is it four more light years? Henderson says you're supposed to let the other runners carry you through the last part of the race. That sounds like a good idea, but there aren't many runners around now. There are some walkers, but they don't help. They discourage me. There's one runner up ahead in a yellow T-shirt, on the back the word "dummy" is printed in blue letters. Does that mean him or me? It could work either way. Grinding out the last four miles with a big blue dummy sign jiggling in front me, now he's slowing down. Don't stop. If you pull me in, I'll push you in. Fair enough. He's walking. I'll have to pass him. Good-bye, brother dummy, see you in the shower.

The water tower is getting closer, though. It's not a mirage. There's an end to this somewhere. Somewhere on the other side of infinite distance, infinite time, maybe when I finish I can lie down and drink the water tower until it's dry, or maybe they can carry me to the top and throw me in. But I have to finish – that's not a choice – I have to finish. I don't know why. I don't care why. Burn what you have to, body, just let me finish. Burn it in the runner's internal fires and send the smoke out the runner's chimney.

Twenty-five miles. Just past the timers, there's a nice looking girl. She asks me if I want some ice. Her smile reflects concern and compassion. We're going to make it, old paint. We're going to fall down, mangy moose, just don't fall down. If I fall down, six men and a crane won't get me up.

Twenty-six miles. Only the stupid 385 yards to go. I think the extra yards came in because some Queen of England didn't want to move to watch an Olympic marathon. I'll finish now. The rest of it could be barbed wire and broken glass and I'd crawl over it somehow. I'd rather finish running, though. Here's the track. It's almost over. Oh, what a beautiful site. There's a great big finish banner to run under. There are people there and some kind of music. If marathoners have a heaven, it must be something like this.[1]

Now let me read to you Knute Larson's parallel for the Christian marathon.

> The start of the Christian life is joyous, after all those years of fighting faith, the spiritual release of beginning the race is a pure high. Like children rushing out for recess, we're finally saved. Some people at work are trying to get me to forget Sundays and join their sports club and they laugh at my faith. I wonder what would happen if all Christians decided to forget the whole thing and just go sit around. Would it spoil some vast eternal plan? Maybe it would. For sure. Ten years and all's well. Try not to think about all the possible temptations if you can help. Test hit. Not everyone is talking and laughing now. Some have dropped out or fallen back. Now and then a wall hits. Satan makes inroads. Life seems like it isn't even worth it. For a few days you even forget that you have the Holy Spirit. It's scary, but you get back to trusting and the running and serving happens again.
>
> A lot of people are walking now. In fact, some of the people who got you started in the Christian life are walking. Some of them are even sitting down. They got tired, they say. A few invite you to join them in the shade, but you can't because you hear the voice of the Lord and the Scriptures calling you. Somehow

in your mind's eye, you see Him running, enduring the worst of affliction, taking even the pain of the cross for you and you want to go on. You ask for the control of the Spirit and you get going, doing what's right. There's one runner up ahead with the word, "hypocrite", printed in big blue letters on his back. Does that mean him or me? It could work either way. Now he's slowing down. He's walking. I'll have to pass him. Good-bye, brother hypocrite.

The end is getting closer. I know Christ will be back some day, maybe when He comes I can lie down and drink from the Water of Life forever in the presence of Jesus Christ, Himself. I have to finish. It's a choice, but I have chosen. I know why—because of all Christ has done for me and the beauty of the finish. I'll finish now, the rest of the race could be tests of all kinds, but I know the Lord will give grace and strength. I'm going to make it. Here's the finish banner and Christ is back. What a sight! And some kind of music! There's my mother and my sister. Hello! Hello! There's David and Paul and all the saints. Jesus, my Lord, I love you![2]

---

[1]Larson, Knute.*Run Steady, Run Straight.*Victor Books, 1990.

[2]Ibid.

Chapter 5

God, Who Comforts The Depressed

2 Corinthians 7:11
August 11, 2002

In 1937, a well-known Bible teacher and pastor by the name of Harry Ironside wrote a book on the subject of biblical repentance. He called it *Except Ye Repent,* and the reason he wrote this book was because he was alarmed at how many of his contemporary preachers were excluding the doctrine of repentance in the message of the Gospel. He began the book with these words: "The doctrine of repentance is the missing note in many otherwise orthodox and otherwise fundamentally sound circles today."[1]

If the doctrine of repentance was a missing note in many pulpits in the 1930s, then we could say it is virtually non-existent among the majority of Christian preachers today. Many evangelical churches never mention the subject of repentance, and yet the message of repentance was a central element of the gospel that Jesus and the apostles preached. For example, in Matthew's gospel, right after our Lord's temptation, Jesus began His ministry, and His first recorded words were: *"Repent, for the kingdom of heaven is at hand"* (Matthew 4:17). Jesus began His ministry by calling Israel to repentance. Later, when the Pharisees questioned why He ate and drank with sinners, Jesus defined the purpose of His ministry by stating, *"I have not come to call the righteous but sinners to repentance"* (Luke 5:32). In other words, Jesus conveyed the message: "If you want to understand what I'm doing here with sinners, it's this – I'm calling sinners to repentance."

The message of repentance was also a recurring theme in our Lord's preaching. That's why he spoke to some very self-righteous people who thought that a certain group of people had died in a catastrophe because these people were greater sinners than they were. And so, in self-righteousness, they spoke to the Lord and asked Him to explain it, and Luke 13:5 states His response: *"Unless you repent, you will all likewise perish."* In other words, the message He expressed there was, "Those people weren't greater sinners than you are. Everyone needs to repent. Don't think that this happened to them because they were really sinful but you're not. *Unless you repent, you will all likewise perish."*

Not only was repentance at the heart of our Lord's message, but in Luke 24 He commanded His followers that they were to preach the gospel of repentance after His death, burial, and resurrection. This is really the expanded version of the Great Commission, telling us what it is that we're actually supposed to tell people. In Luke 24:45 it says *"He opened their minds to understand the Scriptures."* In verse 46 He said to them, *"Thus it is written, that the Christ would suffer and rise again from the dead the third day."* So we are to preach the message of Christ's death, burial and resurrection. But how are we to do that? What do we tell people they need to do in terms of responding to that? Verse 47 goes on to say, *"And that repentance for forgiveness of sins would be proclaimed in His name to all the nations, beginning from*

Jerusalem." The heart of our message, and the apostles' message, is to tell people that Christ has died for their sins and that in order to be forgiven, they are to repent of their sins. The apostles understood that and that is exactly what they preached. Do you remember that on the Day of Pentecost, Peter stood before thousands of grieving Jewish people who came to the realization that they had indeed rejected their Messiah, and with grieving hearts they said, *"What shall we do, brethren?"* (Acts 2:37). Peter, speaking for all the apostles, responded, *"Repent"* (Acts 2:38). There's only one thing to do – repent. And then (and I'm paraphrasing) he added, "You ought to be baptized because you have been forgiven for your sins because you have repented." Later, in Acts 3:19, Peter told another crowd of Jewish people in Jerusalem, *"Therefore, repent and return so that your sins may be wiped away."* Peter preached repentance.

The apostle Paul emphasized repentance in his preaching too. In Acts 17, he confronted the philosophers from Athens, who were pious in their knowledge, and looked down on Paul. Paul concluded his message to the philosophers in verse 30 by saying, *"Therefore, having overlooked the times of ignorance, God is now declaring that all people everywhere should repent."* In essence, Paul was saying that God turned His head away from dealing with them in judgment up until now. But God is now telling everyone to repent. That was Paul's message to the Athenian philosophers.

In Acts 20, Paul met with the elders from the church at Ephesus and explained how he had conducted his ministry to them, and he saidthat he went from house to house and proclaimed the whole counsel of God. Then in verse 21, he narrowed in on the heart of his message: *"solemnly testifying to both Jews and Greeks of repentance toward God and faith in our Lord Jesus Christ."*

In light of the overwhelming evidence that repentance was a central element of the gospel that Jesus and the apostles preached, what does it mean to repent? When the Bible speaks of repentance, it is referring to a change of mind that always leads to turning from sin as we turn to God. And it's important to understand because there are many Bible teachers today who will tell you that repentance means nothing more than an intellectual change of mind.

The reason they say that is because the Greek word for *repent* or *repentance* is made up of two Greek words which, when put together, mean "to change the mind." But that is a bad way to define a term because words are defined based on how they are used in context. You figure out what somebody means based on how they use a word, so you can't isolate a word and say, "Well, it's two Greek words that make one Greek word, so it means 'to change the mind.'" Changing the mind is only part of it, and it's important you understand this because some will say, "Well, changing the mind means 'I used to believe this about Christ; I thought He was just a man or just a prophet, but now I believe this. Now I believe the truth about Him.'" Or, "I used to think I really wasn't a sinner but now I've changed my mind about that," or "I've changed my mind about God." That's certainly a part of it, but that's not the totality of repentance. Repentance is not simply an intellectual altering of our minds, or that I simply "have a new perspective on my sin." Repentance is always preceded by, and always involves, a God-given grief and hatred over our sin. It is a grief that causes us to turn away from our sin as we turn to God for salvation. That's how the Bible uses the term *repentance*.

The proof that this is precisely what Scripture is talking about, that repentance involves forsaking sin and not simply a passive change of mind, is provided by the Bible itself. Acts 26 is the most critical passage in terms of defining that repentance involves forsaking sin. The apostle Paul, in explaining his ministry to King Agrippa, explains that repentance involves forsaking sin, and whenever you have a biblical definition of something, you have the best definition because it carries biblical authority. So this is the most significant definition of repentance in the Bible because it's actually defined for us in the text of Scripture.

In Acts 26:18, Paul is making his defense before King Agrippa and in so doing, he explains the ministry which God had called him to do. He says that his God-given ministry in regard to the Gentiles, *"is to open their eyes so that they may turn from darkness to light, and from the dominion of Satan to God, that they may receive forgiveness of sins and an inheritance among those who have been sanctified by faith in Me."* Paul is saying to King Agrippa that his ministry is to proclaim a message that would turn people from *darkness*, which is another way of saying to turn people from "ignorance and sin" to the *light,* which is another way of saying "Christ and obedience," and he clarified it by saying that what he means is that they were to turn *"from the dominion of Satan"* (their evil ways), and turn *"to God."* That's what Paul said his ministry was. He said forgiveness of sins comes by turning away from sin and turning to God.

But watch this! As he continues to speak to King Agrippa, he actually gives some clarification and a defining statement. He says in Acts 26:19, *"So, King Agrippa, I did not prove disobedient to the heavenly vision,"* and then in verse 20 he goes right back and explains what his ministry was: *"but kept declaring both to those of Damascus first and also at Jerusalem, and then throughout all the region of Judea, and even to the Gentiles that they should repent and turn to God, performing deeds appropriate to repentance."* Notice how Paul, in explaining his own ministry, says that turning from darkness to light, from Satan to God, is called repentance. He defines it for us. That is a very important statement in the Bible because Paul himself defines for us that repentance involves turning from sin and darkness to Christ and to the light. So repentance is more than an idle change of mind that has no impact on our behavior. It is far more than that. It is always preceded by sorrow for sin and always leads to forsaking of our sin. Paul gives us the most significant definition because it's the biblically inspired definition of repentance.

I believe the best, most comprehensive, and thorough explanation of repentance that I have ever read comes from the pen and ministry of Dr. D. Martin Lloyd-Jones, who is a very well-known Welsh expository pastor and Bible teacher. Here's what he wrote:

> Repentance means that you realize that you are a guilty, vile sinner in the presence of God, that you deserve the wrath and punishment of God, that you are hell-bound. It means that you begin to realize that this thing called sin is in you, that you long to get rid of it, and that you turn your back on it in every shape and form. You renounce the world whatever the cost, the world and its mind and outlook, as well as its practice. And you deny yourself and you take up the Cross and you go after Christ. The nearest and dearest to you in the whole world may call you a fool or say you have 'religious mania.' You may have to suffer financially but it makes no difference. That is repentance.[2]

That's a superb quote because it's significantly broadens the definition of repentance for us.

With this background to provide us with a little more understanding, we are ready to approach our study in 2Corinthians 7, because this deals with the subject of repentance. In the final verses of chapter seven, Paul reveals how God had restored his broken fellowship with the Corinthians because they had repented. They had indeed repented of their sin; they repented of the way they had treated Paul, and did something about it. As a result of this renewed fellowship with the apostle Paul, God brought Paul out of depression. He tells us in verses five and six that he was depressed. He says in 2 Corinthians 7:5-6, *"For even when we came into Macedonia our flesh had no rest but we were afflicted on every side, conflicts without, fears within. But God who comforts the depressed comforted us by the coming of Titus."* What he means is that he was waiting in Macedonia—fearful, depressed, discouraged, fearing the worst—afraid that Titus was going to get there, and after meeting with the Corinthians, he would tell Paul, "They don't like you anymore and they want nothing more to do with you." Paul was, at that point, a nervous wreck about the whole matter, and he admitted that he was depressed. But he tells us in verse six that God is the One who comforts the depressed. And what this passage is about is how God comforted, strengthened, and encouraged the depressed apostle Paul and brought him to the place of rejoicing.

He rejoiced with the Corinthians in their response because verse seven says, *"and not only by his coming but also by the comfort with which he was comforted in you as he reported to us your longing, your mourning, your zeal for me so that I rejoiced even more."* Paul said, "I was depressed but I'm no longer depressed, and the reason I'm no longer depressed is because of what Titus told me about your response." This occurred in three phases. First, they longed to have fellowship with him again. What great news! They didn't reject him anymore. They said, "Paul, come back. We want that fellowship restored." Second, they mourned over the way they had reacted to him as a result of his strong letter. They actually wept over that and it grieved them that they actually treated the apostle Paul this way. And, third, they were now zealous in their desire to obey what he had taught them. Everything had changed and Paul was now rejoicing. The

God of all comfort indeed had comforted Paul and brought him out of depression.

In light of this, what Paul does in these last few verses is use himself as a living illustration to reveal how God encourages believers when they're down. Paul gives us several principles about how God lifts us out of depression. The first principle God uses to encourage depressed believers is simply that He renews broken fellowships. One of the most disheartening things in life is to have broken fellowship; the anguish of a severed relationship with someone you once loved, someone you once walked with, someone you once were close with that is now broken. I can't think of anything more painful in life. I can't think of anything more painful than to be estranged from someone that you still love, for-whom you still have feelings.

On the other hand, I don't think there is anything more exhilarating than having that fellowship restored, and that's what Paul is so excited about. That's what Paul experienced, and you and I must never lose hope that God is going to deal with people who are estranged from us, so that there is repentance. Or it may be that we need to repent. I have found that whenever you speak about repentance people think about all the other people who should repent towards them. So we want to keep that in mind, but never lose hope, that God can restore a relationship that's been severed by sin. God did it with Paul and an entire church; He can certainly do it with us and those from whom we are distant—even now.

But how does He do that? How does God bring about this restoration of fellowship? Paul tells us that God not only restores broken fellowship but He also produces repentance in sorrowful Christians. That's how He brings people out of depression. Those they have been estranged from come back to them and it's a wonderful experience. In 2 Corinthians 7:8-10 the Apostle Paul says:

> *For though I caused you sorrow by my letter I do not regret it, though I did regret it for I see that the letter caused you sorrow though only for a while. I now rejoice, not that you were made sorrowful but that you were made sorrowful to the point of repentance, for you were made sorrowful according to the will of God so that you might not suffer loss in anything through us, for the sorrow that is according to the will of God produces a repentance without regret leading to salvation, but the sorrow of the world produces death.*

The recurring theme in these verses is that Paul's letter, known to us as 1 Corinthians, had caused this church great sorrow about which Paul said he was glad. He was not glad because they were sorrowful per se. He didn't rejoice because people were hurting; rather, their sorrow led them to repentance, and that's why Paul was glad. In other words, Paul's joy was over their repentance. It's just that the sorrow had to precede that repentance.

And in verse nine he states that God was behind their sorrow. This didn't just happen; God was behind it. He said that it was according to the will of God. It *"is according to the will of God,"* meaning God was in this; God had worked in their hearts and brought them to the place of grief over their sin that led them to repentance. That's always the way it is. Nobody musters up repentance on their own because we are wicked sinners, dead in sins and trespasses. If there's any repentance in an unbeliever's heart, it's because God has granted them repentance. Unbelievers cannot repent in-and-of themselves just as they cannot believe in-and-of themselves because they are spiritually dead. Because of that, God makes the first move and He grants repentance. And that's what Paul is saying here—that God worked in your hearts and brought you to faith. As a believer, He did this in your life because that's the norm in a believer's life. We repent.

In 2 Corinthians 7:10, Paul clarifies that the sorrow that they experienced was different than the sorrow that non-Christians experience. Look at what he says in verse ten: *"For the sorrow that is according to the will of God produces a repentance without regret leading to salvation, but the sorrow of the world produces death."* Two types of sorrow are presented in this verse: the first sorrow is the sorrow of God-given grief over our sin. Paul says this type of sorrow produces repentance which belongs to the realm of salvation. Literally translated, in the Greek language, it does not say *"leading to salvation,"* though that is certainly true. A better way to put it is that it produces repentance which belongs to the realm, or the sphere or the dominion, of salvation. In other words, he is saying that repentance goes with salvation. Repentance is part of the package. We repented at the time of our initial conversion experience, and the repentance we continue to have on an on-going basis gives proof that we are true believers and have been saved.

The other type of sorrow is what Paul calls *"the sorrow of the world,"* meaning this is the sorrow experienced by non-Christians which does not lead to salvation. The Bible says that eventually it leads to death because it has no redemptive value. It doesn't do anything for us spiritually; it doesn't produce repentance nor lead to salvation. It may relieve us of some tension and stress, but it has no spiritual benefit in our lives which is what Paul is trying to point out here. Ultimately, if people just have worldly sorrow and don't repent, they will die in their sins and go to hell.

Now, as I stated previously, this type of sorrow comes in many different forms but not to be confused with repentance. For example, there is often sadness about getting caught. There are some people who are horribly remorseful and weep bitterly, but it's more of a frustration. It's more of a sorrow because they were caught, and they are frustrated because they would like to have gotten away with their plans, but now that they got caught, everything is messed up. That's not repentance nor is it the sorrow that leads to repentance.

Sometimes the sorrow manifests itself in that we're sorrowful and sorry for the consequences of our sins. There's a deep remorse because we see that our sin has damaged other people and it has damaged ourselves. It may have cost us our job or the joyous family relationship we once experienced and we're very sad about that, but, once again, that's not the sorrow that leads to repentance. That's just sorrow that says, "I feel bad because of what my sin has caused."

Sometimes sorrow manifests itself in the sense of being sad because of shame or embarrassment over bad behavior and the individual feels badly about it, but nothing more—it doesn't go any further than that. This type of sorrow is always bothered by sin, but only on a human level, not on a divine level. It only thinks about "how my sin affected me" or "how it affects other people" and nothing more. It is not bothered by God's attitude towards the sin so there's no vertical-relationship concern. An illustration of this in the Bible is Esau, who sold his birthright to Jacob for a single meal. A birthright might not mean a whole lot to us, but it meant everything to him because it represented the covenant blessing. It's why the Jewish people are in God's sovereign plan as His covenant people and not the Arab people. But Esau sold his birthright because he was hungry. That was a despicable thing to do. In Hebrews 12, we have a divine commentary on Esau and the Bible condemns him greatly for his actions. Please understand that God's sovereign plan was for the birthright to go to Jacob. It was to be Abraham's line through Isaac and Jacob, but that still does not relieve Esau of his wicked behavior and responsibility. So in Hebrews 12:16-17, the writer is warning this church made up of

Jewish people not to be like Esau and he warns them *"that there be no immoral or godless person like Esau who sold his own birthright for a single meal, for you know that even afterwards, when he desired to inherit the blessing, he was rejected."* After he gave up his birthright he wanted it back, and God said, "No." So what did Esau do? He had a temper tantrum, as Hebrews 12:17 goes on to say, *"for he found no place for repentance though he sought for it with tears."* Now you read that and it looks like the Bible is saying that he wanted to repent but he couldn't or that he cried out for repentance but God said, "No," but that's not what it means at all. Esau's tears were not the tears of a repentant man, because he didn't seek repentance. What it means is that he sought the covenant blessing with tears and he did not get the blessing, making them tears of frustration, not tears of repentance. They were tears of frustration because he sold his birthright for a meal and God said, "That's it. You don't get a second chance." He cried about it but it didn't change God's mind. Esau was a man who had worldly sorrow; frustrated over what he had done, but he didn't repent.

On the other hand godly sorrow, the sorrow that leads to repentance and salvation, is characterized by a deep sense of anguish over our sin. We understand that we have sinned against the holiness of God. We have sinned against the Almighty and even if it doesn't impact anybody else, it grieves us because it has grieved God. That is the kind of sorrow that leads to repentance. In fact, this is why Old Testament repentant believers often dressed in sackcloth and ashes. This practice of dressing in sackcloth and ashes is not something we do today, but when it was done in ancient times, those were symbols of mourning and anguish about having sinned against the Almighty. It demonstrated their sorrow in an outward form. That's why Job said to God in Job 42:6, *"I repent in dust and ashes"* after God rebukes Job for thinking he knows what's going on. He doesn't know what's going on and he really doesn't understand God. God said to him in essence, "Were you there when I created the world? Do you know everything?" And Job just replied: *"I repent in dust and ashes."* That's what sackcloth and ashes meant.

What about the repentant Ninevites? They repented at the reluctant preaching of Jonah, which resulted in the Ninevites repenting and mourning over their sin. It says they mourned as they put on sackcloth and they sat on ashes. Although He didn't use the term "sackcloth and ashes," this is what Jesus meant in the New Testament when, in the Sermon on the Mount, He said in Matthew 5:4, *"Blessed are those who mourn for they shall be comforted."* The mourning He was talking about was the mourning for sin. *"Blessed are those"* is directed to believers who mourn because of their sin, who have a sense of deep anguish over their guilt, *"for they* (the believers) *shall be comforted."*

Now I want to stop here and apply this because I think it is absolutely critical that we understand that repentance is an essential ingredient for coming to Christ for salvation. No one ever came to Jesus Christ for salvation who didn't come with a repentant heart. It's absolutely imperative to understand this concept, so let me put it this way: All those who come to Christ come by way of repentance and faith, as repentance and faith are two sides of the same coin; they go together. There is a point in time in which we come to Christ for salvation, but there is a process that leads up to that, and the process always begins when we come under the conviction for our sin, whereby God shows us how sinful we are. We're not just a little sinful, rather we are totally infected with sin, so much so that we're contagious. That's what the Bible means by total depravity: Every part of us is depraved even if we don't behave as wickedly as we could behave. We are fallen in every part of our being, and we come to the realization of how wicked and sinful we are, which leads to conviction. We grieve over our sin and we're bothered by it, but not because it's messed up our lives. We may indeed be bothered about it, but primarily we grieve over our sin because we recognize that God is holy and we have sinned against the holiness of God. Finally, we turn away from our sin as we turn to Christ to save us. That, in a nutshell, is the repentance-faith process.

When I came to Christ as a freshman at the University of South Florida, I didn't know what *repentance* or *conviction of sin* meant; but what I did know was that I was a sinner. God had shown me that I was a sinner and I knew that I didn't want to continue in my sin. I knew that I hated the way that I was living, and I didn't want to continue living that way and so I came to Christ. I didn't understand all of this, but I came to Christ because God had worked in my heart. When God brings about repentance—and He alone is the One who grants that—we mourn over our sins. Even if you don't understand all that's going on, you mourn over sin. You hate and turn from your sin. That's what's involved in all of this.

There are many individuals who attend evangelical churches in America who claim to know Christ, and yet they have never repented of their sin. I emphasize "in America" because if you go to other countries and visit Bible-believing churches, you find that they understand repentance. In fact, I am told that in Russia the word *repentance* is used synonymously for being saved, so if they are saved, they are a *repentant one*. It's part of the whole transaction and they understand this. In our American evangelical churches, we don't preach repentance or else we have distorted and watered it down. There are many individuals who are either members of or identify with evangelical, fundamental churches, yet they have never repented of their sin because they never hear about this in their churches. These are the people who I'm very concerned about (which is why I'm preaching this today) who feel like they have "asked Jesus into my heart. I'm safe. That's all that matters. I've given a few words of invitation and some counselor told me I was saved and that's it, so I don't need to be concerned about anything else. I'm going to go to heaven. I can live any way I want to live because Christ died for me and that's all that matters." But that is not what the Bible teaches.

Walter Chantry, in his book *Today's Gospel: Authentic or Synthetic*, refers to people like this who profess to be Christians but live like they're non-Christians. He speaks of those who "add Jesus as personal hell insurance for the world to come."[3] That's their attitude: "Jesus is your hell insurance. He's your 'Get out of hell free' pass." That's basically what it boils down to. But those who believe this way are not saved! And if you're in this category, I don't want you to be deceived into thinking you're saved. I don't want to stand before the Lord and have Him say, "Steve, you never preached on repentance. You had hundreds of people who listened to you weekly and you didn't warn them or tell them the truth, and you were responsible as their shepherd." So I'm telling you these truths now.

John 3:16 is the most famous verse in the entire Bible. It tells a person, in summary form, how to be saved, *"For God so loved the world that he gave his only begotten Son that whoever believes in Him should not perish but have eternal life."* But John not only tells us how to be saved, but a few verses later, starting in verse 19, we're told why men and women are not saved. *"This is the judgment, that the light has come into the world and men loved the darkness rather than the light,"* Why? *"For their deeds were evil. For everyone who does the evil hates the light and does not come to the light for fear that his deeds will be exposed"* (John 3:19-20). John is telling us that people don't come to Christ because they are not willing to forsake their sins that have been exposed by the light of Christ. That's the bottom line.

Because I'm Jewish, people will often ask me, "Can you explain how come the Jewish people, for the most part, to this day have rejected Christ?" The answer is that it's the same reason why most Gentiles to this day have rejected Christ; men love darkness rather than the light, and they come up with all kinds of reasons why they haven't come to Christ. The real reason is because Jesus exposes their sin and they're not willing to repent. That's exactly why Jews and Gentiles don't come to Christ. They would prefer to walk in darkness so they can continue carrying out deeds of darkness.

How do you know if you've ever really repented of your sin? How do you know if you've truly been born again? Don't ever assume that you are because you were raised in a Christian home, you prayed a prayer, and you've been in a church like ours for many years, that you are born again. So how can you know for sure? One of the proofs that you're really saved is that you continue to repent of your sin on a daily basis. In other words, you feel badly when you sin. You are grieved about it. You are bothered when you sin and you confess your sin to God. Confession of sin is not simply saying, "God, I'm sorry that I did this." Confession implies that not only are you sorry about it but you do not to want to continue in it. Confession always involves a repentant heart. You may still struggle with that particular sin, and you may fall into it from time to time; in fact, you may fall into it a lot, but you hate it. As a believer, you must hate it and want to forsake it for the sake of Christ. If you don't have that attitude, you're not a believer. If there's not ongoing repentance in your life, you have a legitimate reason to question whether you have really come to Christ. It's important to understand that repentance is not a onetime experience that takes place at your conversion. Repentance only starts at your conversion and then one of the proofs that you have truly been converted is that you continue to repent over your sins in your life as you grow in the Lord. In fact, that's part of the growth process. The Lord shows us all the time how sinful we are; if He didn't show me my sin on an ongoing basis I wouldn't have much of a prayer life.

This brings us in our study to 2 Corinthians 7:11 which is very important because it states: *"For behold, what earnestness this very thing, this godly sorrow has produced in you. What vindication of yourselves! What indignation! What fear, what longing, what zeal, what avenging of wrong! In everything you demonstrated yourselves to be innocent in the matter."* This is a significant verse because it shows us what the godly sorrow of the Corinthians actually produced in terms of repentance. If you want to know what repentance looks like in terms of the fruit of repentance, this is it. Paul shows us, based on the Corinthians' repentance, the change of attitude that takes place in all believers who repent. This is important in terms of practical life because it helps us to know if someone truly has repented. If someone comes to you and says, "I'm so sorry. I feel badly about what I did and I'm sorry," how do you know if they're really repentant? Anybody can say anything because talk is cheap. How do you know if they're truly repentant, or if they just feel badly because it made you feel badly? How do you know if it's true repentance or worldly sorrow?

Allow me to be more specific: If you have an estranged spouse who wants reconciliation and he or she says they feel badly about what they've done and they want to get back together, how do you know whether it is real repentance or just worldly sorrow? Second Corinthians 7:11 tells us what to look for so we will know if there is genuine repentance. Let's consider another example: How can our elders know if a disciplined church member has truly repented? If the church disciplines someone and they say that they have repented, they have to tell our elders that. They have to come and meet with the elders and this is what they are going to be looking for in that person. They can't just take somebody's word for it because anyone can say, "I feel badly and I want to come back to the church. Reinstate me as a member." So how can we tell if anyone claiming that they're sorry for their sins has genuinely repented? Verse 11 is the key to what we're going to do. Without going into too much detail and taking too much time on this, we're just going to highlight the eight marks that Paul gives of true repentance as demonstrated by the Corinthians. This is what the fruit and attitudes of true repentance looks like. If you see these attitudes demonstrated in someone, it's true repentance. If these attitudes are not there, it's not true repentance, so don't be naïve and gullible about it.

The first clause of 2 Corinthians 7:11 says, *"For behold what earnestness this very thing, this godly sorrow, has produced in you."* The first evidence of repentance for the Corinthians was their earnestness, which means eagerness or diligence. The point is, they were eager to get things straightened out with Paul. It was the first thing they wanted to do so; they didn't delay but instead, they made haste to resolve the matter. So, the first evidence of genuine repentance is a diligence to aggressively pursue righteous behavior. When you're convicted of your sin and you repent, you aggressively pursue righteous behavior.

It reminds me of the principle Jesus spoke of in Matthew 5:23-24. He said, *"If you are presenting your offering at the altar, and there remember that your brother has something against you, leave your offering there before the altar and go; first be reconciled to your brother, and then come and present your offering."* In other words, Jesus said, "Leave your gift, get up, and get things right with your brother." This is the type of eagerness Paul is talking about. Don't continue worshiping because this is far more important than your worship. God doesn't accept it anyway, so go and get right with that other person.

Any person who says they've repented but still has just sort of a casual indifference to sin, has not repented. If they have the attitude of "Yeah, I know I'm wrong. I know I shouldn't have done this and I know I need to get things straightened out, but I just haven't gotten around to it yet" – that's not repentance. That may be some form of legalistic standard or obligation imposed upon someone who merely says, "Yeah, I'm going to do it," but that's not real repentance. When God brings us to repentance, we can't wait to get it straightened out and we do not let another day go by. That is a proof of genuine repentance: an eagerness to do what God wants us to do. Those who repent are passionate about it and are determined to get things straightened out with God and with other people as necessary.

Second, the subsequent attitude that demonstrates repentance is from the next phrase in verse 11 which states, *"What vindication of yourselves!"* The word *vindication* means "defense" or "apology." The thought here seems to be that the Corinthians were eager to clear their name by apologizing to Paul and to God for their sin; they wanted to get things straightened out. They recognized that they had brought shame on the name of Christ, shame on their church, shame on their testimony, and had hurt Paul deeply. They wanted to clear their name by asking forgiveness. This is a very vital part of repentance; a truly repentant person will humble himself. Whatever it takes to ask forgiveness—not only from God, but if there's been another person involved, he goes to that person and asks his forgiveness. In this case, the Corinthians needed to ask Paul's forgiveness for the way they had treated the apostle. The sure sign of repentance on our part would be to make things right with any individual that we've sinned against. It's humbling and sometimes awkward, but this is what it takes. Remember what Lloyd-Jones said: "Whatever it takes." No matter what people say, no matter how odd you may feel, you do it – you ask their forgiveness.

Third, Paul continues with the next mark of repentance. The next phrase in verse 11 says, *"What indignation."* When he says *"what,"* it's sort of like us saying, "Wow, I'm impressed." Paul didn't just say, "They're indignant." No, it's "What indignation!" It's an exclamation, such as, "What earnestness! What clearing of their name! What indignation!" The *indignation* he's talking about is "anger." It's righteous indignation. The Corinthians were angry and indignant at their own sin and their own behavior. They looked at the way they had acted in their treatment of the apostle Paul and were righteously indignant at themselves over their sin and the shame it had brought to the Lord's testimony at their church. Anyone who has ever repented understands that there is a holy hatred towards their own sin, and it grieves them to think that they have treated the Lord this way and that they've treated other people this way; they simply hate their sin. That's why I'm saying that this is not a casual indifference. It's not "when I get around to it, I might get it straightened out"—that's not repentance. If you display any of these qualities of indifference or lack of concern about your sin, you're not a believer because when God brings salvation to us He gives us a new nature, and that new nature is constantly dealing with us through the Holy Spirit about sin. We are constantly seeing our own depravity and having to ask God's forgiveness, and we grieve over our sin, because we rejoice in forgiveness but we grieve over our sin.

Fourth in verse 11, Paul emphasizes, *"What fear!"* The Corinthians had a new, healthy attitude; a wholesome fear towards God. We don't often speak about the fear of God but there is a legitimate reverence towards God as the one who disciplines us. And we say, "Lord, I love You, but I also have this incredible fear that You're going to discipline me and I don't want that." This is something you always want to look for in someone who says they have repented. Do they recognize that their sin has offended God and do they now have a new attitude of honoring and pleasing the Lord? There ought to be a wholesome fear—"I did this. God dealt with me. I don't want to do this again. And I fear if I do it again God is going to discipline me even harder."

Fifth, Paul expresses. *"What longing!"* The Corinthians longed for Paul to visit them so that they could get things right with him face to face. They yearned to make it right! That's the thought here—the yearning to be restored to fellowship with the apostle; a consuming desire. Do you have that? When you're estranged from people, do you have that? Do you have that longing to have things straightened out? When you've sinned against somebody, does it bother you to the point that you think, "I can't even wait another day; it's such a yearning in my heart. I can't stand being out of fellowship with that person. I can't stand that things are not right with us." That is the mark of true repentance.

Sixth, Paul says, *"What zeal!"* This probably refers to the Corinthians' zeal to honor Paul as an apostle by obeying his teaching. What this means in practical terms is that if you have mistreated someone and you repent, your repentance will be demonstrated by a new zeal in treating the person properly. If you treat them in the same rotten manner that you treated them before, it's not repentance. Repentance isn't "Well, I'm sorry I mistreated you and I think I'll do it some more. I just feel bad about it". If you don't change and have a new zeal towards honoring them and treating them differently, you have not repented.

The seventh mark of repentance is, *"What avenging of wrong!"* The thought here is that the Corinthians wanted to see justice carried out, even if the justice and punishment was for their own sin. Whatever it took to have justice meted out—even if it hurt. It may very well be that Paul is referring to a specific incident here because he mentions, at the end of this verse, something about *"the matter."* So it seems that there may be one specific incident in Paul's mind to which he is referring, in addition to their general avenging of wrong. And that one wrong would seem to be the man whom the church disciplined because he was having an incestuous relationship with his stepmother. Back in 1Corinthians 5:1-2, Paul did not rebuke the man, but rather he rebuked the church for being so lenient and tolerant with the fellow, and said, "Put him out! You can't let that stuff go on in the church. Put him out!" They apparently did that because we read in 2 Corinthians 2 that he appeared to have repented and so Paul now says, "Forgive him." But it also seems to me that Paul is saying, "You dealt justly. You had justice carried out." The application is, if you're truly repentant you don't try to remove the consequences of your own sin. You just take it on the chin—whatever the consequences are. Don't try to squirm out of justice by saying, "Well, I've repented so do I still have to go through this?" Yes, you do, regardless of the cost or justice meted out.

Finally, eighth, he says, *"in everything you demonstrated yourselves to be innocent in the matter."* This is the bottom line; it proves someone has truly repented. They demonstrate the reality of their repentance by taking the steps necessary to correct things. So Paul says, "You're no longer to be blamed. You're no longer one who we can point a finger at. You're innocent in this." How can you tell if someone has really repented? They'll do more than tell you that they're just sorry. They will demonstrate a real change of heart by making changes in their behavior and attitudes.

We opened our study by quoting from a well-known Bible teacher and pastor of another generation, Harry Ironside, who was concerned about the church's lack of preaching repentance in his day. I want to close our study with a quote from a well-known Bible teacher and pastor of today who is equally concerned about preaching that is void of the doctrine of repentance. In his book *Faith Works*, John MacArthur wrote these profound words:

> I am deeply concerned as I watch what is happening in the church today. Biblical Christianity has lost its voice. The church is preaching a gospel designed to soothe rather than confront sinful individuals. Churches have turned to amusement and show business to try to win the world. Those methods may seem to draw crowds for a season, but they are not God's methods and, therefore, they are destined to fail. In the meantime the church is being infiltrated and corrupted by professing believers who have never repented, never turned from sin, and, therefore, never really embraced Christ as Lord or Savior.[4]

Could you be one of these people who identifies with the church, associates with Christians—you know the language, you speak the evangelical jargon—and yet you've never repented? And the proof that you've never repented is that sin doesn't bother you. You may have a rotten relationship with your spouse and a rotten relationship with your children. You know things are not right in your life, but you just let it slide. I think that you should be very concerned if that's been your lifestyle because it may very well indicate that you've never come to Christ.

You know who was like this? A man in the Bible who identified with believers but was not a believer, and that was Judas Iscariot. Judas, who for three years ate, drank, lived and served with all the apostles and yet Jesus called him the Son of Perdition—unsaved, lost, doing what he was doing, thinking everything was fine. I want to make sure, as best I can, to warn you that you do not live like a Judas; that you're not just among us, taking it all in, but sin has never really been dealt with in your life. If you've never come to

Christ with repentance and faith, I urge you to do this. We often hear people say things like, "Well, I did that." which means, "I asked Jesus into my life and nothing ever happened." That's because those are just words. But you speak them as if they were 'magical words'—"Jesus, come into my heart." What does that mean? When a person comes with deep contrition over their sin and comes and bows at the Cross and says, "Lord, I know that I'm a wicked sinner and I know I deserve hell. I don't want to live like that. I don't want to live in rebellion to you anymore. I know that Christ died for my sins and I trust Him with all of my heart," that is a person who has just met the Savior. If you're not one of those, I urge you to do that because God commands men everywhere to repent.

Where do you stand on this issue? Are you someone that John MacArthur was talking about? Infiltrating the church, professing to be a believer, but you've never repented, you've never turned from sin? You've never really embraced Christ as Lord nor have you embraced Him as Savior? If so, I urge you to turn to Him as only God can grant repentance. But I don't want you to have a false assurance. You need to trust Christ. Cry out to Him for mercy and salvation.

For those of you who do know Christ, I want to give you as much biblical assurance as possible. If you repent of your sin and you're bothered by your sin and you don't want to continue, and you forsake your sin—even if it's a struggle, that's a sure sign that you know Christ because that is the repentance that is part of salvation. That is how you can have evidence your salvation. Paul said, *"He who began a good work in you will perfect it"* (Philippians 1:6). That good work is not salvation alone; that good work also involves repentance—it began at salvation and it continues. So if you are repenting of your sin, then I encourage you to continue in that.

And I want to say to those who are sitting here and know that things are not right with someone else; they've been estranged, and the relationship is severed...be like the Corinthians and repent over that. Ask God to forgive you and go to the people who you've sinned against and ask them to forgive you. It may very well be that you think, "Well, they're wrong too." Listen, they have to stand before God and you're not responsible for what they do, but you are responsible for what you do. Even if there's just 1% that is your responsibility and 99% is theirs, take care of that one percent responsibility that you have and repent.

Lord, Your Word pierces us because it is sharper than any two-edged sword, and your Word can get into areas that nothing else can because it can reveal thoughts and the intent of our hearts. Lord, I would pray that your Word indeed would have its deep effect upon us today.

I pray, Lord, for those who may be like Judas associating with believers, even members of the church, but never have they really repented and trusted Christ; I pray that they'll be made aware of this. And, Lord, I pray for those who are believers that You'll continue to show us areas we need to repent of that we might know on a daily basis the joy of fellowship that comes from being clean and right before You.

I would also pray for those who may be estranged from loved ones. I pray that they'll do everything they can, like the Corinthians, to get it right with that person and they won't put it on the other people to do what they need to do, but they'll do what You're calling them from Your Word to do. I pray that they will know the thrill that comes from restored fellowship.

We pray this all in Jesus' name, Amen.

---

[1]Ironside, Harry.*Except Ye Repent*.American Tract Society. 1937.

[2]D. Martyn Lloyd-Jones.*Studies in the Sermon on the Mount*.(Grand Rapids: Eerdmans, 1959).2:248.

[3]Chantry, Walter.*Today's Gospel: Authentic or Synthetic?*Banner of Truth. 1970.

[4]MacArthur, Jr., John F.*Faith Works*. Dallas: Word Publishing. 1993. 85.

Chapter 6

THE BELIEVER'S RELATIONSHIP TO THE LAW
Introduction to the Ten Commandments
October 26, 2003

Some time ago, my wife Michele and I were invited to a friend's home for dinner. Our host informed us that she was also inviting a Jewish friend to join us that night with the hope that I, as a Jewish follower of Christ, would be able to witness to her friend from a Jewish perspective. And so I did. That night I spent a great deal of time trying to be culturally relevant to this Jewish woman as I presented the Gospel with a Jewish flavor. I emphasized the Jewishness of Jesus. I emphasized the Old Testament messianic prophecies which were fulfilled only in Jesus of Nazareth. I told her about the Jewish flavor of the New Testament and that all of the Lord's first followers were Jewish.

That evening was a very pleasant experience. This lady did not argue with me, nor did she raise any serious objections. There were no tense awkward moments. Everything went well. In fact, it went too well. This unsaved Jewish woman found no problem with anything that I shared nor with me personally. She found no problem with what I told her about Jesus. In fact, she basically agreed with everything I had to say. From all appearances, it looked like it was a very successful evening of witnessing. But it was not. It was not at all a successful evening of witnessing.

When Michele and I got in our car to go home that evening, I said to her, "You know, I really blew it tonight. I was so concerned about relating to this woman as a Jewish person that I failed to emphasize that she was a sinner. That's the heart of the message, that people are sinners and need salvation. What I should have done was told her about the Law of Moses and specifically the Ten Commandments in order to help her to see that she is a lost sinner and in need of salvation. Instead I'm emphasizing all this stuff about being Jewish. That's so secondary. She's a sinner first. That's what I should have done." I told Michelle, "Do you know what I need to do? I really should teach a series on the Ten Commandments so that we can all clearly identify God's holy character and the true nature of our own sinfulness."

And so, out of my own failure to effectively witness to a Jewish woman that night was born a new study on the Ten Commandments. It is a study for which all of us have a critical need because without an accurate understanding of the Ten Commandments not only will we fail to identify God's holy character and the true nature of our sinful condition, but we will also fail in presenting an accurate Gospel picture, and accurate Gospel message to others. You see, it is only through the preaching of the Law as the expression of God's holy character that people come to see themselves as fallen, wretched creatures. The Law defines for us the specifics of our sin.

In fact, that was how Jesus evangelized people. Do you remember the rich young ruler who came to Jesus and said, "What must I do to inherit eternal life?" What did Jesus do? He presented the Law to him. He said, "Have you done this? And have you done that?" That was our Lord's perspective.

The Master Evangelist presented the Law to this man so this man would see his own sin, the sin of coveting—a violation of the tenth commandment.

He did the same thing with the Samaritan woman. After speaking with her about giving her living water, she begged Him to give it to her. Instead, He said, "Go tell your husband." And she said, "I really don't have a husband." He said, "You're right. You've had five husbands, and the man you're living with now is not your husband." What was our Lord doing? He was putting His finger on her sin of adultery, just like He put His finger on the sin of the rich young ruler.

And so our Lord used the Law in evangelism. As Walter Chantry so graphically put it, "Only by the light of the Law can the vermin of sin in the heart be exposed."[1] And so, if the Law reveals and exposes our sin, it is important for us to realize that any evangelistic effort must at some point proclaim God's Law. Certainly not as a means of salvation—that would be heresy. That would be salvation by works. Everything in the Bible, both Old and New Testament cries out against that. But as the way to show people the true nature of God's holy character, and also the true nature of our sinful character. That's the purpose of the Law.

It was Martin Luther, the German reformer, who once said, "The law must be laid upon those that are to be justified, that they may be shut up in the prison thereof, until the righteousness of faith come—that, when they are cast down and humbled by the law, they should fly to Christ. The Lord humbles them, not to their destruction, but to their salvation. For God woundeth, that he may heal again. He killeth, that he may quicken again."[2]

You see, it is only when an individual sees his sin that he realizes his desperate need for the cross of Christ as an atonement for his sin. But he has to see himself first as a sinner before he'll see his need for a Savior. In fact, we could say that the preaching of the Law is really the first message of the cross because without the moral standards of the Law revealing God's holiness or revealing our utter depravity, our sins don't really seem to be a serious problem to us. We adopt the attitude, "Well, I'm a sinner, you're a sinner; it's no big deal." But unless we see the serious problem of being a condemned sinner who has broken God's Law and that there is a penalty for doing such, then we're really not going to be too concerned about needing a Savior to deliver us from our sin. And that's why the apostle Paul told the Galatians, *"Therefore the Law has become our tutor to lead us to Christ"* (Gal. 3:24). The Law points to Christ. In other words, the Law teaches us the truth about ourselves, teaches us the truth about God's holiness, teaches us the truth that we need a Savior, and teaches us that we cannot keep the Law. It is impossible to keep the Law. You may be able to keep the externals of the Law but not the moral intent of the Law which is an inward attitude of obedience; not simply external behavior.

And once again the words of Martin Luther in explaining the value of the Law are worth considering. He writes:

> As long as a person is not a murderer, adulterer, or thief he would swear that he is righteous. How is God going to humble such a person except by Law? The Law is the hammer of death, the thunder of hell, and the thunder of God's wrath to bring down the proud and shameless hypocrites. When the Law was instituted on Mount Sinai, it was accompanied by lightening, by storms, by the sounds of trumpets to tear to pieces that monster called self-righteousness. As long as a person thinks he's right, he's going to be incomprehensibly proud and presumptuous. He's going to hate God, despise His grace and mercy, and ignore the promises in Christ. The Gospel, the free forgiveness of sins through Christ, will never appeal

to the self-righteous. This monster of self-righteousness, this stiff-necked beast needs a big axe, and that's what the Law is, a big axe.³

And that is precisely why the apostle Paul made some of the most profound statements concerning the Law. For example, in Romans 3:20 he said, *"Through the Law comes the knowledge of sin."* And in Romans 7:7-8 on a personal note about his own life, he said, *"What shall we say then? Is the Law sin? May it never be! On the contrary, I would have not come to know sin except through the Law; for I would not have known about coveting if the Law had not said, "You shall not covet. But sin, taking opportunity through the commandment, produced in me coveting of every kind; for apart from the Law sin is dead."* Then, in verses 9-10 he said, *"I was once alive apart from the Law,"* meaning, "I thought everything was okay with me. I performed all the ceremonies. I kept the external observances. I went through all the ritual cleansings. I thought I was okay." He wasn't alive spiritually, but he thought he was.

Then he said, *"but when the commandment came,"* meaning, "It came to my heart; the Spirit of God applied it to my life. I understood what the Law really meant." But then, *"...sin became alive..."* meaning, "I thought I was alive, but the Law aroused sin in me." *"And I died,"* meaning, "I was slain. I was killed. The Law condemned me. I realized I was a dead sinner; dead spiritually"—*"and this commandment, which was to result in life, proved to result in death for me."* It is through the Law that knowledge of sin comes to us.

Yet, as important as the Law is in evangelism and to show us our need for Christ and to define personal holiness, too many Christians minimize the importance of the Ten Commandments. There are a host of reasons why this is so, but one major reason is because they've been told by some Bible teachers that the Ten Commandments are irrelevant to us as church-age Christians. Some teach that the Ten Commandments were only relevant to Israel, because they were under the Law, but not to us. Some teachers in the Dispensational camp teach such. They say that we are no longer under Law but under grace, and they interpret that to mean that the Ten Commandments were strictly for the nation of Israel, not for church-age believers today. According to this view, the Ten Commandments may lead you to Christ, but once you come to Him, you are not biblically mandated to obey them. They are irrelevant in your life.

One of the most influential teachers of this view was Lewis Sperry Chafer, one of the founders of Dallas Theological Seminary, who was highly influenced by C. I. Scofield who developed the Scofield Reference Bible. In Chafer's mind, every dispensation had to be either under the rule of grace or the rule of Law, but never both. He wrote this, "Both the age before the Cross and the age following the return of Christ represent the exercise of pure Law, while the period between the two ages represents the exercise of pure grace."[4] What he means by that is that Israel had pure Law, no grace. The kingdom following this day and age, the church-age, will be the Messianic or Millennial kingdom. He says it will be characterized by pure Law again; no grace. In between is this age—the church-age, the age of grace, or whatever you want to call it—but Chafer would say that this is the age of pure grace, no Law; that you cannot have them mingling together. That's what he is saying here.

He writes, and I continue, "It is imperative, therefore, that there shall be no careless co-mingling of these great age-characterizing elements else the preservation of the most important distinctions in the various relationships between God and man are lost, and the recognition of the true force of the death of Christ and His coming again is obscured."[5] In other words, he saying that before Christ came, believers were strictly under Law, but now we're strictly under grace.

When He returns and establishes His kingdom, He will again rule again strictly by Law. In Chafer's theological system, there was no room for grace and Law to exist together.

Now please understand that I believe that Lewis Sperry Chafer was personally a godly man. But he opened the door with this theology for many who would follow his teachings to legitimize a style of Christianity characterized by careless and carnal behavior. This is at the heart of the "lordship salvation" issue. Many who hold to the system of theology known as dispensationalism are in opposition to the doctrine of Christ's lordship. This is not true of all who are dispensationalists, but some are opposed to the idea that submission to Christ's lordship is a part of true saving faith, because in following Chafer's brand of dispensational teaching, they see grace in opposition to all biblical Law. And so when they come to the New Testament, their perspective on personal holiness and obedience is that it is merely an option. It is not a demand.

And so they would say that grace makes only suggestions and Law makes only demands. And since we are not under Law but under grace, the Ten Commandments become only suggestions. And this is what leads some in this movement to make such statements as, "You can trust Christ as Savior, and later on—it's optional—you can decide whether or not you will submit to him as Lord." This is at the heart of the issue because they do not mix Law and grace.

Now, I want you to know that theologically, I am a dispensationalist. But I'm a dispensationalist in the sense that I believe that the Bible makes a clear distinction between the promises made to Israel and the promises made to the Church. The two groups are not the same. But I do not for one moment believe that the Bible teaches that being under grace frees me from keeping the Ten Commandments. Nor do I think that grace eliminates the need for believers today to keep the moral laws of God.

So, the real question we face is, how do we theologically balance statements in the Bible that say we are under grace and not under Law with keeping the moral standards of the Law expressed by the Ten Commandments? This is a critical issue. This is one of the most critical and difficult issues to really grasp. What is the relationship today between grace and Law? Before we begin to examine the Ten Commandments we have to understand this first before we can see that the Ten Commandments are relevant for us, that we are mandated to obey them, that they're not something we just read and say, "Oh, that's for Israel and not for us, and I don't need to obey them."

If we don't arrive at a biblical balance and understand the relationship of grace to Law, then we'll fall into one of two extremes. We may fall into the extreme of antinomianism, a theological term which means "no law," which is a viewpoint that provides us with a license to sin. It's the attitude that says "Once saved, always saved; do whatever you want. You'll never lose your salvation." The Bible doesn't teach that, but there are some Bible teachers who teach that it says that. So if we're not careful, we will say, "We're no longer under the Law, so therefore, we can do whatever we want." That is antinomianism. That is a license to sin. Jude speaks about that concerning false teachers—they promote a license to sin.

Or, we may go the other extreme and say, "Everything is under the Law. All of the laws are in effect." And if you do that, you've got the same problem that the apostle Paul faced in the early church. This was the crisis of the early church. Jewish people came along in the early days of Christianity and said, "Look, you've got these Gentiles coming to faith in Christ. They need to obey the Law. The men need to be circumcised. They need to keep every Jewish festival. They need to go through all of the ritual cleansings. They need to keep all of the holidays. They need to eat only kosher foods."

And the apostles fought against that, and in every one of Paul's letters he fights that. That's called "legalism," and in Galatians Paul refers to that view as *"a different gospel"* (Gal. 1:6). Paul was the strongest defender that salvation is by grace alone through faith alone and that it was unnecessary to keep the Law. But ultimately, if you say you have to follow the Law, you end up in legalism. So it is critically important that believers understand this issue of the relationship of law and grace.

There are two vital truths about the Law, and specifically the Ten Commandments, that will keep us from these very dangerous, erroneous extremes. If you think, "Well, that's just an ancient issue; nobody really believes that we have to obey all of the Law today," let me tell you, they do. As someone who is Jewish, I've been exposed to a lot of Jewish believers in the Messianic Jewish movement who would say that. They would say, "Yes, we are under Law. You've got to obey all the Jewish holidays. You've got to obey all of the Jewish dietary laws. Don't you dare have ham! Don't you dare have sweet and sour pork! You can't! It's prohibited." So this is a very relevant issue. There are even those who want to go back to all the civil laws that Israel had, and they believe our government should follow those laws.

The first vital truth about the Law of Moses that protects us from error is the permanence of the Law. That was God's intention. Let's look at Matthew 5:17-18. In light of how many Christians believe that grace releases them from the obedience to the Law of God, it is fascinating to note that Jesus said just the opposite. He said that the Law had an abiding and permanent nature. Look at what He said here in verse 17: *"Do not think that I came to abolish the Law or the Prophets; I did not come to abolish, but to fulfill."* He is saying, "I didn't come to destroy them. I didn't come to replace them. I didn't come to set them aside."

Verse 18: *"For truly I say to you, until heaven and earth pass away, not the smallest letter or stroke shall pass from the Law, until all is accomplished."* Now the question is: Why would Jesus feel compelled to mention that He had not come to abolish or to nullify or destroy the Law? There's a reason for this. The Sermon on the Mount, of which these verses are a part, was directed at Christ's followers. He said that right at the beginning of the sermon in Matthew 5:1-2. It says, *"When Jesus saw the crowds, He went up on the mountain; and after He had sat down, His disciples came to Him. He opened His mouth and began to teach them."* So this is a sermon for disciples, for believers.

All of this ties in with what I told you about the teaching of Chafer and Scofield and their followers, because since Jesus went on to speak about the Law, they say that the Sermon on the Mount is irrelevant for Church-age believers too. They say that since He spoke about Law, this is for the messianic, millennial kingdom. It's for the Jews after the church-age. But that simply isn't so because in this sermon Jesus spoke about false prophets and false teachers, and things that will not exist during the millennial kingdom. So this is for believers. Jesus was saying, "In light of the fact that the kingdom hasn't come, how should you live?"

So, why would Jesus feel compelled to mention about not destroying the Law? One reason was that His followers often heard from the Jewish religious leaders that Jesus broke the Law. He didn't, but they said He did. The religious leaders accused Christ of doing such things as failing to keep their interpretation of the Sabbath law because He dared to heal someone on the Sabbath. He dared to do good on the Sabbath, and because of their very narrow interpretation of the Sabbath law, they said, "He's a Sabbath breaker. He's a law breaker." So Jesus had to defend Himself against that.

Additionally, Jesus didn't teach Law-keeping as a way of meriting salvation. That's what the Jewish religious leaders taught. In fact, in Matthew 5:20, Jesus said, *"For I say to you that unless your righteousness surpasses that of the scribes and Pharisees, you will not enter the kingdom of heaven."* In other words, the Pharisees thought that by being good and keeping the Ten Commandments, they were going to get to heaven. Jesus said, "You'd better have something far better than that," and what He meant was, "You need to have My righteousness put on your account because you don't have any righteousness of your own. You're not keeping the Law." My point is that Jesus didn't teach what they taught. He taught that He was the way to heaven, not Law-keeping. This was new to them, so Jesus needed to clarify it.

In addition, when Jesus did refer to the Law, He did not give the traditional, rabbinical interpretation. He spoke as one with authority and He gave the true intent of the Law. They thought He gave His own unique Galilean interpretation, as if He was modifying or replacing the Old Testament Law. Notice Matthew 5:27-28. Jesus said, *"You have heard that it was said, 'YOU SHALL NOT COMMIT ADULTERY'; but I say to you that everyone who looks at a woman with lust for her has already committed adultery with her in his heart."*

What Jesus was saying was, "You've heard from all of your teachers that the commandment, 'You shall not commit adultery' simply means that if you have not committed the physical act of adultery, you have not broken the Law. But I'm telling you—as the One who gave the Law, the divine Son of God, the Lawgiver—that the intent of the Law was never simply the physical act alone. It's a part of it, but it also means what is going on in your heart, in your thoughts. It goes far, far beyond the externals."

So Christ was not saying, "I'm changing it." He wasn't modifying the Law. He was saying, "This is the way it always has been, though you didn't know it. You didn't understand it." And so to dispel any doubts and confusion as to where He stood concerning the Old Testament Law, Jesus makes this profound statement in verse 17 about not coming to destroy the Law or the prophets, which means the entirety of the Old Testament. *"Law"* in this context does not refer only to the Ten Commandments. It means the first five books of the Old Testament, the Law of Moses. And *"the Prophets"* refers to the remainder of the Old Testament inspired writers. It's everyone else who wrote Old Testament Scripture. So Jesus meant the whole Old Testament. Instead of coming to replace the Law with new laws, Jesus said that He actually came to fulfill them. And in verse 18 He added that these laws will never pass away. They are permanent and they will all be fulfilled, or take place. That's essentially what *fulfill* means—to complete, to take place.

What did Jesus mean by that? In what way did He fulfill the Old Testament Law? The apostle Paul gives us great insight into this. In Galatians 4:4 he said, *"But when the fullness of the time came, God sent forth His Son, born of a woman, born under the Law."* We often look at that verse and say, "Yes, Jesus was born as a Jew." It certainly does mean that, but it means far more also. It means that though He was the eternal Son of God, He came into this world as one who perfectly obeyed the Law of God in every one of its aspects. He came as one who subjected Himself to the very laws that He laid down. The divine laws that you and I find impossible to keep because of our sinful natures, Jesus kept. He kept every one of them and He kept them perfectly—all of them. He kept them as our legal representative, as our substitute. In other words, what we couldn't keep, He kept in our place.

There are a number of statements about that in Scripture. In John 8:29, Jesus said this, *"And He who sent Me is with Me; He has not left Me alone, for I always do the things that are pleasing to Him."* Jesus was saying, "I always obey His laws. Everything I do, the Father is pleased with because I perfectly obey His laws." In John 8:46, He said, *"Which of you convicts Me of sin?"* That's a great question! "You have all kinds of problems with Me. What sin have I committed?" And nobody could answer because He never committed any sin. And in Psalm 40, a Messianic psalm, David is looking ahead prophetically to the Lord Jesus, and in verse eight he writes concerning Christ, *"I delight to do Your will, O my God; Your law is within My heart."* Jesus not only perfectly obeyed every aspect of the Law, He delighted to do that. He enjoyed it. He lived for that. That was His food. That was His drink. That was what His life was about.

But Christ not only fulfilled the Law by obeying it in our place by His perfect life, but He also fulfilled the Law by obeying it in our place by His death on the Cross. You see, the Law demands that if we break it, there must be punishment. Not just physical punishment, but eternal punishment. It is the condemnation of the Law. It causes the one who is judged to be cursed forever and ever. The Law demands that sin be punished. That's why Scripture says, *"For the wages of sin is death"* (Rom. 6:23), and what that means is that the penalty for breaking the Law is death, both physical and eternal, which the Bible refers to as hell. Eternal separation from God – that's how holy God is and how sinful we are. That is the just demand of the Law. Therefore, because Jesus Christ was our legal representative, in fulfillment of the Law, He died for our sins. He died in our place. That's why Scripture says, *"He made Him who knew no sin to be sin on our behalf, so that we might become the righteousness of God in Him"* (2 Cor. 5:21). In Christ's death, God treated Jesus as if He had broken all of the Law, even though He had never broken any of the Law. Why? Because He was our legal representative and we have broken the Law. But on the cross, God treated Him as if He broke all of the Mosaic laws, and when we come to Christ and trust Him as our Savior and Lord, He treats us as if we have perfectly kept the Mosaic Law, all of it.

The righteousness we receive at salvation that is credited to our account is the righteousness of Christ in perfectly obeying the Law. It is not His intrinsic righteousness as deity, but rather the righteousness of perfectly obeying the Law. God looks at the believer in Christ as one who has perfectly obeyed the Law. That's why there's no condemnation for us. It's not just that our sins have been paid for. That's part of it, but it's also that God has placed on our account the very righteousness of Christ in keeping the Law. He doesn't look at us as lawbreakers anymore. Christ obeyed the Law in our place and took the punishment and condemnation for disobeying the Law. That is the epitome of mercy. That is ultimate grace. Therefore, when Christ said that He had come to fulfill the Law, He meant that He is the fulfillment of every part of the Law.

All the laws point to Him. He is the very embodiment of the Law. When Jesus said "I have not come to destroy the Law but to fulfill it," it's in the same sense as prophecy. He didn't come to destroy prophecy. He saying, "I'm the embodiment of it. It all points to Me, and I fulfill it." That's the sense here. All the laws pointed to Him, and by His life and death He fulfilled every one of them.

Now the Law is broken down into three aspects. First of all, there are the ceremonial laws. Those are the laws such as the sacrificial system, the Levitical priesthood, the Jewish feasts, ceremonies, dietary laws, ritual cleansings, temple worship, and so forth. Those were ceremonial laws. All of those ceremonies were merely symbols and pictures of Christ. He is the reality. He is the substance. They were types and pictures. They pointed to Him. We are not obligated to keep these laws. That's the message of the book of Hebrews. That whole system is placed aside because in Christ it was done away with, in the sense that He fulfilled them. He is the fulfillment.

That's why in Colossians 2:16 when Paul was dealing with the efforts of the legalists to put others under the bondage of legalism by telling them what was required on certain days and what foods they could eat, he wrote, *"Therefore no one is to act as your judge in regard to food or drink or in respect to a festival or a new moon or a Sabbath day."* Those are the ceremonial laws. Then notice what he said in verse 17: *"things which are a mere shadow of what is to come, but the substance belongs to Christ."* They're only shadows. They're only pictures. They were fulfilled in Jesus Christ. He indeed is our Passover. He is our cleansing. He is our Sabbath rest. He is our ultimate sacrifice. He fulfilled all of that. You are no longer under any law to eat certain foods. You can choose whatever you want to eat, but those things are for nutritional purposes, not religious purposes. It may not be good for you, but you are not under any Old Testament rule of life as to what you can eat and you can't eat. And the same thing applies to Jewish holidays and feasts.

In Acts 10:9-16, God gave Peter a vision of all kinds of animals, both clean and unclean, on a great sheet descending from heaven. He said, *"Get up, Peter, kill and eat"* (v. 13). In other words, "Eat whatever you want, Peter." God said that to an orthodox Jewish man who had never eaten anything unclean. And when Peter protested, the Lord said, *"What God has cleansed, no longer consider unholy"* (v. 15). God was simply saying that those aspects of the ceremonial laws are done away with in the sense that they're fulfilled in Christ. Jesus didn't destroy them. He simply fulfilled them.

Secondly, Jesus also fulfilled all of the judicial laws or civil codes that governed Israel. These are laws about justice, and Christ fulfilled them because He is the epitome of justice. He is just! He is perfectly righteousness. But there is also a sense in which He fulfilled them in that the cross marked Israel's rejection of the Messiah. These civil codes were for Israel, specifically how to govern Israel. And the cross marked Israel's rejection of the Messiah. By virtue of that rejection, God has temporarily—not permanently—but temporarily set Israel aside as He builds His church today, made up of Jew and Gentile.

The New Testament makes clear that the church is not mandated to follow these civil laws and legal codes. Someone may ask, "How do you know that?" Because, if we were, then we are mandated to take stubborn, rebellious children out and stone them to death. That's what the legal code said. Anyone who has ever been involved in adultery is to be taken out and killed. That's the legal code of the Old Testament.

Instead, what the New Testament teaches is that we are to abide by the judicial code set down by the government under which we live. That's the lesson of Romans 13. If you happen to live under a government that says those involved in adultery are to be killed, then that's what happens in that land. But we're not in that land, and the point is that we don't live by those civil laws. We are not Israel. That was uniquely for Israel. But the judicial laws and the ceremonial laws were all fulfilled in Christ in the sense that in His death they're done away with for us.

But the important question for us is this: What about the moral laws which are presented in outline form in the Ten Commandments? Are we still obligated to obey them? And the answer is emphatically and dogmatically, "Yes." Why? Because the moral laws are an expression of God's unchanging holiness. The way Jesus continues to fulfill those moral laws today is by writing them in the hearts of His people through the ministry of the Holy Spirit. He is still fulfilling them through us.

This is taught in Romans 8. In Romans 7, the apostle Paul speaks about his own struggle with the law, and he tells us that he is a sinner. I am convinced Paul wrote this as a believer. He desires to obey God in his inner man but he struggles with it. The things he doesn't want to do, he does. The things that he wants to do, he doesn't always do. And so it is a struggle. He comes out of Romans 7 into Romans 8, and in verses 3-4 he says, *"For what the Law could not do, weak as it was through the flesh, God did: sending His own Son in the likeness of sinful flesh and as an offering for sin, He condemned sin in the flesh, so that the requirement of the Law might be fulfilled in us, who do not walk according to the flesh but according to the Spirit."*

Do you realize what Paul is saying? He is saying because of our sinful natures, the Law was powerless to either save us or produce any righteousness in us. The Law doesn't have that ability. That's not the purpose of the Law. But through the death of Christ, God's condemnation against sin was poured out on His own Son.

And now the very moral laws of God that we once were unable to obey, that we once hated, we are now able to obey them because the Holy Spirit has changed our hearts. And even though we still struggle with sin, we have the power to obey them, and the desire is there to obey them as well.

What Paul is referring to here by implication is a promise given long ago to Israel and applied to us in Jeremiah 31:33. It is called the New Covenant. We entered into the aspect of the New Covenant when we came to faith in Christ. Jesus established the spiritual aspect of the New Covenant when He established the Lord's Supper. It is the New Covenant in His blood. Now it does have a future, full fulfillment to Israel also, but look at what Jeremiah said: *"But this is the covenant which I will make with the house of Israel after those days,"* declares the LORD, *"I will put My law within them and on their heart I will write it; and I will be their God, and they shall be My people."* God has placed His Law in our hearts. The morality of the Law always continues.

Sinclair Ferguson wrote this: "God's law is no longer an external rule that we find burdensome, because God has given us a new heart, committed to Him and His ways. We want to obey Him. That's often one of the first discoveries a new Christian makes. Whereas before He struggled against God's Law, now he finds that he has a heart to obey it."[6] What he is saying is that is the evidence of the new birth. The new birth is regeneration. The new birth is God's nature in you. You have been given a divine nature and that is why we say if someone claims to know Christ and yet has no desire to obey Him, he doesn't truly know Christ. The evidence of being a believer is not that you perfectly obey, but that you have a desire to obey, that your life is characterized by obedience. That's the message of the book of First John, and for that matter, that's the message throughout the Bible.

The point of this is to say that the Ten Commandments are the eternal expression of God's will for believers in every age. They were not introduced to mankind at Mount Sinai when God gave them to Israel. Most people don't realize that. Long before God ever revealed the Ten Commandments to Israel in written form, they were written in the hearts and in the consciences of everyone. That's what Romans 2 teaches.

Romans 2 is in a passage in which Paul proves that everyone on the planet has suppressed the truth of God. They may not have all of the Bible in written form, but whatever they knew about God, they suppressed. They said, "We don't want it. We're not going to obey it. We're not interested." Then he puts the Jew on trial and says, "You have the Law but you haven't obeyed it." He puts the Gentiles on trial and he says, "You have the truth about God but you haven't obeyed it."

Now where did the Gentiles get the truth? Remember, he's talking about pagans. Romans 2:12— *"For all who have sinned without the Law will also perish without the Law, and all who have sinned under the Law will be judged by the Law,"* meaning, even if you don't have the Law in written form, you're going to perish if you don't obey the truth.

How would they know the truth? Verse 13— *"for it is not the hearers of the Law who are just before God, but the doers of the Law will be justified."* That's true. If someone could keep all the Law, they would be justified. But there's only one who has done that, and that's Jesus.

Verse 14— *"For when Gentiles who do not have the Law"*—meaning they don't have the written Law—*"do instinctively the things of the Law"*—he's talking about the Ten Commandments now, that is, the moral aspect of the Law— *"these, not having the Law, are a law to themselves, in that they show the work of the Law written in their hearts, their conscience bearing witness and their thoughts alternately accusing or else defending them."* What he is saying is that though not everyone knows the Ten Commandments by name, everyone knows intuitively in his own heart and conscience what is right and what is wrong. There's a moral code written in our hearts. There is an innate awareness of what is right and wrong, and when unbelieving pagans who have never read the Bible, and have never seen anything of the Ten Commandments violate these moral laws, they experience the weight of a guilty conscience.

They can get callous to that, but they know what guilt is. Why? They don't have the written Law, but they do have the Law in their hearts. That's always been the way it is. That's why the Bible, even before the giving of the Law, presents Bible characters as having a knowledge of sinning against God. Remember Joseph in the Old Testament who was in Potiphar's house and Potiphar's wife tried to seduce him and drag him into bed with her? And he said, *"How...could I do this great evil and sin against God?"* (Genesis 39:9). How did he know that was a sin against God? He had never read, *"You shall not commit adultery."* It was in his heart and so he knew that.

Cain knew that it was wrong to kill his brother Abel. Abraham knew that it was wrong to lie about Sarah being his sister. Jacob made statements about knowing that stealing was wrong. These individuals knew that. They didn't need the Law to tell them that. The Law simply codified all of the morality that God had put in the heart. The Ten Commandments articulated it. It was really a very gracious thing for God to say, "Let Me spell it out to you clearly." But the truth has been given to all of us. And the moral laws are still binding on us today. They existed before the Law was given to Israel, and they continue to exist today.

And that's why they are mentioned throughout the New Testament. In fact, in Ephesians 6, when Paul speaks about children obeying their parents, he said, "That's what the commandment says, *'Honor your mother and father.'*" Paul speaks as if the Commandments are in operation today, because they are. They were always intended by God to be of a permanent and lasting nature.

The question one might have is this: "Doesn't Paul say that we're not under Law but under grace?" Yes, he said that, but what did he mean? He meant that we are no longer under any moral obligation to keep all the ceremonial and civil laws. We are no longer under that type of a system. We have been set free to live under the system of grace. But grace doesn't free us from keeping God's moral laws. So the first vital truth that keeps us on track and away from error is that the Law is permanent in nature.

There is a second truth I will cover briefly. The second truth that keeps us from error is this: The Law—specifically the Ten Commandments—has an ongoing purpose in the life of a believer. We understand from the New Testament that no one can ever be saved by keeping the Law. Romans 3, Romans 10, and Galatians 3 speak of that. To say anything else is heresy. You cannot be good enough by keeping the Ten Commandments to get to heaven. No one is able to keep them in accordance with their true intent.

But once we turn away from the Law as a means of salvation, and we place our faith in Christ, Jesus sends us back to the moral laws and says, "Now, obey them out of love – not trying to merit heaven, but because you love Me."

A man came to Jesus one day and he said, "What is the greatest commandment?" What did Christ say? *"'You shall love the Lord your God with all your heart, and with all your soul, and with all your mind.' This is the great and foremost commandment. The second is like it, 'You shall love your neighbor as yourself.' On these two commandments depend the whole Law and the Prophets"*(Matt. 22:37-40). That's what it's all about. Love God and obey Him. Love and Law go together. It's the same thing as saying grace and law work together. In other words, we keep His commandments because we love Him, and we love others. If you love Him, you will have no other idols in your life. If you love your neighbor, you won't covet his wife. That's what the commandments are about. They're about love, and obedience to God's moral law reveals our love for Him and our love for people.

There is another use of the Ten Commandments in our lives, and it is the one which I spoke of at the beginning of this message, and that is in presenting the Gospel. An understanding of the Ten Commandments and a proper use of them will keep us from giving a distorted picture of the Gospel. We need to use the Law to help people define sin in their lives. They are not sinners in general. They are sinners in specifics. And that was how Jesus used it in dealing with a young, wealthy man.

Let me show you this in Mark 10. This is very important. This passage tells us about a rich, young ruler. He was a young, wealthy man who had some authority. In verse 17, it says, *"As He was setting out on a journey, a man ran up to Him and knelt before Him, and asked Him, 'Good Teacher, what shall I do to inherit eternal life?'"* Do you realize what an incredible question that is? That's as if you were sitting on an airplane and the person next to you said, "Do you know how I can be saved? How can I have forgiveness of sins?" That's incredible! But notice what Jesus said in verse 19: *"You know the commandments.'Do not murder, Do not commit adultery, Do not steal, Do not bear false witness, Do not defraud, Honor your father and mother.'* "What was Jesus doing telling him about the commandments? Since salvation is by grace, why was He giving him the commandments? Jesus certainly knew he couldn't get to heaven by keeping the commandments. That screams in the face of everything the Bible teaches.

But there was a reason why He said this. Verse 20—the rich, young ruler said, *"Teacher, I have kept all these things from my youth up."* Jesus knew that he couldn't get to heaven by keeping the Commandments, so why did He bring up them up? Because this man didn't know he couldn't earn his way to heaven. Jesus also knew that this man had not kept the Ten Commandments, but this man didn't know that. He was self-righteous. Listen again to how he answered Jesus: *"Teacher, I have kept all these things from my youth up."* He's saying he's never had a lustful thought, no lustful fantasies in his mind, never hated somebody enough to murder them, never stole anything. This man was self-righteous.

And so what did Jesus say? He put His finger on his sin. Verse 21 says, *"Looking at him, Jesus felt a love for him* (which, by the way, indicates that Christ loves even the unbeliever) *and said to him, 'One thing you lack: go and sell all you possess and give to the poor, and you will have treasure in heaven; and come, follow Me.'"* Our Lord was saying, "Sell all your possessions and give to the poor," and what He was doing is putting His finger on the Tenth Commandment and saying, "Young man, *'you shall not covet,'* and you are covetous. You are a greedy, rich boy. You are guilty of a covetous, greedy heart, and you need to see yourself as a lost sinner in need of salvation. When you do that, you turn away from the love of riches, that idol you've created in your life called 'money and things,' and then *'come, follow Me'* as your Savior and Lord. That's how you receive eternal life."

That is the same thing we ought to be telling people. We ought to be telling them about their sin specifically, and you do that by holding the Law up and then telling them to turn from their sin. That's repentance. First, conviction, then repentance from sin. And then tell them about the cross, and that's faith in Christ and commitment to Him as Lord and Savior. That's the Gospel message in a nutshell!

For the first time, this self-righteous man had his sin exposed, and he saw his attitude towards money for what it really was—an idol. The Law and the Lawgiver had enlightened him as to his sinful condition. Why do I say that? Because verse 22 says, *"But at these words he was saddened, and he went away grieving, for he was one who owned much property."* He was saddened because he now knew the truth, that he was covetous. But he was not willing to turn from his sin.

What about you? As we begin this series on the Ten Commandments, do you know that you're a sinner? Not just in a general sense that says, "Oh yeah, I have some faults." Do you know that you've broken every one of the Ten Commandments? If not outwardly, you've broken all of them inwardly, and probably a lot of them outwardly. You've broken them as well as I have, in thought and attitude and action. You have idols in your life of which you need to repent. The Law is the axe that's chopped at our lives and drives us to Christ. Let Christ save you today. If you've never come to Him, come to Him today. He died in the place of sinners, taking the penalty of the law, and He will give you His righteousness. Let's bow together for prayer...

Father, we thank you for Your Word. Lord, we delight in Your Word as believers. We would never teach that the moral code is over. God forbid that we should teach that, Lord, because that would be saying that You've changed. So, Father, as we embark upon this wonderful journey of getting into each of the Ten Commandments, we pray that You'll help us to first of all understand that they are not irrelevant for us. They are not for some prior dispensation or some future dispensation. They are for us. They have always been for Your people. They have always expressed Your holy standards.

And I pray, Lord, that as You shine the light on our sin, that You will help us, Lord, not to make excuses, not to justify our sins, but to repent of them; to be honest before You, to confess our own sin, and, Lord, to be in awe of Your holy standards. And I pray that we will be those who proclaim the Gospel, Lord, by preaching the Law, showing people that they are sinners. So many times, Lord, we speak to those who are self-righteous. They think they're good. They can't even name the Ten Commandments but they think they've obeyed them, and they haven't.

And I pray that You will help us, Lord, to be changed in our own lives and in our Gospel witnessing as a result of this series.

If some are here, Lord, today without Christ, I pray that You will shine the light of Your morality upon them that they might see their darkened conscience, their darkened sinful natures, and that they might come running to Christ as the precious One who died for sinners. And we pray this in His precious name. Amen.

---

[1]Chantry, Walter.*Today's Gospel: Authentic or Synthetic?*Banner of Truth. 1970.

[2]Luther, Martin.*Commentary on Galatians.*Kregel Publications. 1979.

[3]Ibid.

[4]Chafer, Lewis Sperry.*Grace.* Zondervan. 1922.

[5]Ibid.

[6]Ferguson, Sinclair.*The Christian Life: A Doctrinal Introduction.* 1981.

Chapter 7

Blessed are Those Who Mourn
The Sermon on the Mount:
Characteristics of True Discipleship
January 9, 2005

This morning we will continue our study of the Sermon on the Mount, examining one of the most unusual statements Jesus ever made. It is found in Matthew 5:4 in a part of the section of Scripture known as the Beatitudes, or the "Blesseds" of the Sermon on the Mount. Jesus said in Matthew 5:4, *"Blessed are those who mourn, for they shall be comforted."*

When we read this, it doesn't sound right to us. The reason it doesn't sound right is because this beatitude is a paradox. A paradox is a concept in which two truths are mentioned that appear to be at odds with one another but actually they are not—they only appear to be; that is what a paradox is. So we read this and ask, "How can someone be blessed if they mourn? What does mourning have to do with blessing?" We might think it should read, "Blessed are they who do not mourn," but instead it says, *"Blessed are those who mourn."*

Someone has defined a paradox as a truth that stands on its head calling for attention. That is what this verse is. It is designed to grab our attention by startling us and it startles us because it appears to be contradictory and impossible. How can those who mourn be blessed because the concepts of blessing and mourning seem to be poles apart? They don't seem to connect at all. It would be more compatible with human experience to rewrite this beatitude with the words, "Blessed are those who have no tears at all." That's how we would like to have it come out. But that is not what Jesus said. He said, *"Blessed are those who mourn."*

In the Beatitudes, the word and concept of "blessed" is not synonymous with "happy"; rather, it speaks of God's approval: it speaks of His smile and His favor upon us. So all of these Beatitudes are explaining to us the sense that we have God's approving smile and that citizens of His kingdom have His approving smile. So here He says, "Those who mourn and grieve are blessed with God's approving smile." And yet that seems so far from the philosophy of the world that we live in because the philosophy of our world is to do everything to forget your troubles; we know we have problems but we don't want to be reminded of them. We certainly don't want to mourn and grieve and cry. We want to do as that old song says: "Pack up your troubles in your own kit bag, and smile, smile, smile." That is the approach of the world.

The means by which people avoid mourning is evidenced by overindulgences of entertainment, pleasure, drinking and drugging problems away in a world overdosed by amusements and distractions. Therefore, when someone comes along whose life is characterized by mourning instead of partying, the world considers them odd, peculiar, and different. They don't want anyone to pour cold water on their party. But being different, being odd, being peculiar is exactly the point that Jesus is making, because that is the message of the Sermon on the Mount.

The primary, central message of the entire sermon is that true believers, citizens of Christ's kingdom are different—different than religious hypocrites and different than secularists. We are different in the way we behave and different in the way we conduct ourselves because we are different in our very inward character. We have been made that way by virtue of the new birth; we have been transformed in our hearts, that is, our innermost being—our core. We are distinct in our essential makeup, and our nature has been changed so that the way we behave is based on inner transformation.

So what Christ is doing in the Beatitudes is clearly expressing how Christians are different than non-Christians. There are no commands or prohibitions here; there are just statements of fact: this is the way believers are. So in this second Beatitude, Jesus is specifically telling us that believers in Him are mourners, we are grievers; we are those who lament and we are those who cry. This is in contrast to unbelievers who do everything they can to keep from mourning, Jesus tells us that our lives are characterized by it. The parallel passage found in Luke 6:25, Christ's words are more striking than they are in Matthew's account because there, Jesus heightens the distinction between believers and unbelievers by saying this, *"Woe to you who laugh now."* He is not talking about an occasional laugh or having a good sense of humor. He is talking about a life that is characterized by laughter or amusement. He says, *"Woe to you who laugh now, for you shall mourn and weep."* In other words, those outside of His kingdom are described as those who laugh in this present world. But in the future, those who laugh now will mourn and weep; but those of us who are now in His kingdom as mourners will be comforted.

That is the way the world is: the world laughs. The world's philosophy is, "Eat, drink and be merry for tomorrow we die. Why wouldn't I want to be happy? I don't want to be reminded of sad things. There are problems all over the world so don't remind me about it." And so the challenge facing us, as we dig into this very brief Beatitude, is to discover exactly what Jesus meant by the concepts that come out of this Beatitude. We do not need to look at what *blessed* means because we already established that it means "to be approved by God." But what are the concepts of mourning and comfort of which Jesus speaks? What we want to discover is what Jesus meant by the phrase *"Blessed are those who mourn."*

I find it very helpful in studying a subject such as this, which is not easy to understand, is to first eliminate wrong interpretations: in other words, what does it not mean? As we eliminate incorrect interpretations, we can begin to see what Jesus does mean. Let me begin by stating what Jesus did not mean by the phrase *"Blessed are those who mourn."* First, He did not mean that His followers should never laugh or enjoy themselves. The reason we know that is true is because the rest of Scripture affirms such. There are statements in Scripture that speak of laughter and joy in our hearts, so Jesus did not mean, and never said, "Don't laugh." This Beatitude does not say, "Blessed are the gloomy and cheerless." There are some Christians who act like that, but that is not what this says. He didn't say, "Blessed are those who are miserable and never laugh." As wonderful as the Puritans were, some of them had some distorted views about this issue, but Jesus didn't say that. Tasteful humor and laughter are presented in Scripture as positive things.

Solomon said in Proverbs 17:22, *"A joyful heart is good medicine."* It is good for you to laugh, but I am not talking about the world's sick, sinful sense of humor. So the right kind of laughter is good. Proverbs 15:13 says, *"A joyful heart makes a cheerful face."* One of my professors at the Moody Bible Institute, who was also a dear friend, Irvin Robertson, used to say to me, "If you have the joy of the Lord in your heart, please notify your face." That's a good reminder. The New Testament even contains a letter centered on the dual themes of joy and rejoicing. That letter is called Philippians, and the basic message of Paul to the Philippians is this: Do not let anyone or any circumstance rob you of the joy and peace in Christ that God has given you. So we know from these other Scriptures that Jesus couldn't possibly be stating in this Beatitude that citizens of His kingdom are characterized by a joyless, grim Christianity that has no cheerfulness in it at all. He couldn't be saying that because that would contradict other Scriptures, and God cannot contradict Himself.

Secondly, Jesus did not mean "Blessed are those who sorrow over the general difficulties and heartaches of life." Now it is true that we sorrow over those things, but that is not what our Lord is talking about. Despite our world's distaste for mourning, there are certain legitimate, valid sorrows from which you cannot get away; you cannot get away from it because they are common to mankind. It doesn't matter about your spiritual condition, whether you are a believer or an unbeliever; you grieve. Regardless of your spiritual condition, you will experience at some point, the grief that comes with the death of a loved one. You cannot avoid this as this is the way of life. Job spoke about being born into trouble; that is the way of our world—troubles often lead to mourning and tears.

We have all mourned over such things as illness, physical pain, financial loss, extreme disappointments with people and things, loneliness, discouragement, the loss of a job, and the list goes on and on. We understand that as these are all natural, legitimate causes of sadness and sorrow; but that is not the mourning that Jesus is referring to here. How do we know that? The mourning that He is talking about in this Beatitude has to do with that which is distinctively Christian; not the mourning of the world in general, but that of Christians—it is reserved only for the followers of Christ. That is the whole point of the Sermon on the Mount, and the whole point of the Beatitudes. Christ defines for us the unique character makeup of citizens of His kingdom, and if He was speaking only about sorrow in general, that would miss the point so He cannot be talking about that. Rather, He is referring to a type of mourning which is unknown by unbelievers as it is foreign to them. It is a mourning that is distinctly for citizens of His kingdom. It is the kind of mourning to which unbelievers cannot relate; unbelievers don't do it: in fact, they aren't capable of it—but we are.

What might that mourning be? The mourning and grieving to which Jesus was referring is a spiritual mourning. It is of a spiritual nature, just as that which is found in the first Beatitude. The first Beatitude says, *"Blessed are those who are poor."* That is not referring to financial poverty; it is not a physical issue, it is a spiritual issue. It is talking about spiritual poverty; being spiritually bankrupt before God.

So also the second Beatitude has nothing to do with mourning over the natural, physical events of this life. In other words, what Jesus means when He says, *"Blessed are those who mourn"* is "Blessed are those who mourn over sin." By that brief statement, Jesus is telling us that one of the defining marks of a true child of God and a citizen of His kingdom is that we are broken-hearted over sin—first our own sin, and then eventually, the sins of others. That is why I say there is a natural flow and logical sequence to the Beatitudes; they are not thrown together haphazardly. There is a natural order and that is why this Beatitude follows being *"poor in spirit."* The only people who are capable of mourning over their sin are those who have first seen their utter depravity and spiritual bankruptcy. That is the natural flow, not only of the Beatitudes, but also of the Christian life.

The Christian first recognizes his poverty of spirit because He sees how righteous God is; then he sees that in light of God's righteousness, he has no righteousness: he is a spiritual beggar. He does not come strutting up to God; rather, he comes as one who has absolutely nothing to commend him before God. He is convinced in his mind that he is spiritually bankrupt, destitute, with no righteousness whatsoever to offer the Almighty.

Secondly, he responds emotionally to his spiritual poverty by mourning over his deficiency; that is, mourning over his sinfulness. In other words, once you discover that you are a spiritual beggar, you grieve over it. You grieve because your spiritual poverty leads you to see how utterly wicked you are before a perfectly holy God, and that leads you to grieve over your rebellion towards Him. You don't grieve simply because you understand that if you don't trust Christ you are going to end up in hell; that aspect is present, but it is also grief over your wickedness. You see your own heart and you see God's mercy, love, and holiness, and it grieves you, as well it should. This is the experience of every true believer. No one comes into the kingdom without an honest sense of his own spiritual corruption and without mourning over that corruption. There are no "non-mourners" in the kingdom; if you do not mourn over your sin, you are not in the kingdom.

That was the experience of Isaiah the prophet. Isaiah 6 tells us of his experience as he saw a glimpse of God's holiness. In verse 1 he said, *"In the year of King Uzziah's death I saw the Lord sitting on a throne, lofty and exalted, with the train of His robe filling the temple."* God gave Isaiah a vision of Himself in the temple—lofty, exalted, and holy. Verse 2 says, *"Seraphim stood above Him, each having six wings: with two he covered his face, and with two he covered his feet, and with two he flew."* A seraph is a category of heavenly angels, and these seraphim could not even look at God because He is so holy. Verses 3-4 go onto state: *"And one called out to another and said, 'Holy, Holy, Holy, is the*

L*ORD* *of hosts, the whole earth is full of His glory.' And the foundations of the thresholds trembled at the voice of him who called out, while the temple was filling with smoke."* Notice Isaiah's response in verse 5—he has seen a glimpse of God in His holiness and his response is, *"Woe is me, for I am ruined"*, which is grief in heightened form. He continues, explaining why he is grieving— *"because I am a man of unclean lips and I live among a people of unclean lips, for my eyes have seen the King, the Lord of hosts."* When Isaiah saw a glimpse of God's magnificent holiness, he was a broken man.

Job had the same experience—and he was considered the best man of his time, not the worst man—yet he suffered so much because he was the best man. He was the godliest man of his time, and yet his eyes were opened to see truths about God he had never seen before, and at the end of the book in Job 42:5-6 he said, *"I havē heard of You by the hearing of the ear; but now my eye sees You; therefore I retract, and I repent in dust and ashes."* In other words, Job says, "I have heard of you God, but now I have seen You in a way that I never saw You before, and so I repent in dust and ashes." That is grieving over sin. When shown the holiness and grace of God, we mourn over our own sin. We not only see how wicked we are, we lament. We travail, if not in outward tears, certainly in internal tears. D. Martyn Lloyd-Jones explains it this way:

> To mourn is something that follows of necessity from being poor in spirit. It is quite inevitable. As I confront God and His holiness, and contemplate the life that I am meant to live, I see myself, my utter helplessness and hopelessness. I discover my quality of spirit and immediately that makes me mourn... But obviously it does not stop here. A man who truly faces himself, and examines himself and his life, is a

man who must of necessity mourn for his sins also, for the things he does.¹

Every true believer enters the kingdom with tears. The Bible does not say that it has to be outward, physical weeping, but always there are internal tears of sorrow for our many sins against God. It is not a casual entrance; you enter weeping.

These are the tears of repentance that Paul pointed out to the Corinthians in 2 Corinthians 7:10 where he said, *"For the sorrow that is according to the will of God produces a repentance without regret, leading to salvation."* He has just finished telling them that there are tears and sorrow that are not the result of genuine repentance. Some people are sad over their sin, but it is often sadness over being caught in the act of sin or over the consequences of their sin. However, a citizen of the kingdom is grieved over his sin whether he is caught or not; whether other people know about it or not. He is grieved because he understands who God is and because he has offended a holy God. It has nothing to do with personal embarrassment or a fear of being caught. I remind you of Judas who was very sad over what he did in betraying Jesus, but there was no true repentance. Esau was very sad, and even wept, but there was no true repentance. But this is the sorrow of genuine repentance which leads to salvation. In other words, when we come to Him—contrite and broken in heart because we see ourselves for what we truly are—that is the kind of sorrow to which Jesus is referring. We see ourselves as we really are—proud, irritable, bad-tempered, angry, jealous, lustful, and mean-spirited. We see those things and we hate them and we are bothered by those sins. They cause us deep grief and anguish because we know that we have grieved and offended a holy and loving God.

How deep and intense is this mourning? We need to be careful that we don't minimize it and soften the blow. This is not an occasional touch of sadness that Jesus is talking about; rather, He is talking about a deep heartfelt grief, a deep, inner agony. I say that is because the particular word that is used here in the Greek language which is translated "mourn" is a very strong word. There are nine different Greek words used in the Bible for sorrow or tears or similar concepts. This word is the strongest of all those words and it is used to describe the deepest and most heartfelt, gut-wrenching grief. In fact, this word is often used in the Bible to describe the grief that comes with the death of a loved one. So this type of mourning, over sin to which Christ was referring, is as deep and intense as it can be. It is not a casual, once-in-a-while, mild touch of sadness.

At this point we need to get very specific about what we mean by mourning over sin. There are some people who would acknowledge they are sinners, but they are very vague about it. They cannot tell you particularly how they have sinned; instead, it is just a general, vague, obscure acknowledgment of their sin; but, it is impossible to mourn over ambiguous sins: it is impossible to mourn over a general category of sins. When Jesus said that life in the kingdom involves mourning over sin, He meant that there ought to be specific sins that bother us, not a vague category of sins. It is not to be a generic "Yes, I'm a sinner" or "Yes, I agree to a doctrinal statement that says we are all sinners." No, He is talking about definite, specific sins; that is the mark of a true believer. Unbelievers never face their sin, but true believers do. True believers don't excuse or justify their sin; they don't blame others for their sin; rather, they take responsibility for it just as David did in Psalm 51: David didn't blame Bathsheba for bathing on her roof. He didn't say, "Well, she ought to know that I would have been out here. What is she doing?" He said specifically in Psalm 51:4-5, *"Against You, You only, I have sinned and I've been a sinner from the very moment of conception."* —that is the mark of one who really knows the Lord.

One of the ways you can know if you are truly a regenerated, converted Christian is that a true believer no longer rationalizes away sin, but acknowledges them; they grieve over them very specifically. They do not come to God and say as they confess their sins, "God, if I have sinned against you..." When I hear people do that, I think, *"If* you have sinned? Man, name them! That's what the Bible means when it says, *"If we confess our sins."* To "confess" your sin in the Greek language literally means "to agree." If I agree with God, I say, "Yes, I'm a liar. I haven't just lied; I'm a liar. I don't have a little problem with pride; I'm proud." That is the type of confession to which the Bible refers.

Romans 3 amplifies this principle whereby the apostle Paul puts the world on trial and proves that all have sinned, both Jews who have the Law and Gentiles who did not have the written Law but had the Law in their hearts. They have a conscience so they know they have broken God's law. In Romans 3:10, Paul arrives at the climax of his argument and he begins to tell us how we have sinned. This is a picture of all of us. If left to ourselves without any restraints from society or a fear of consequences, we would all behave like this and take it to the nth degree. In Romans 3:10-12 he says, *"There is none righteous, not even one; there is none who understands, there is none who seeks for God; all have turned aside, together they have become useless; there is none who does good, there is not even one."*

So the first thing we see about ourselves is that our soul's very disposition is to go our own way and disregard God's way. That is the heart of sin—to be independent, to do our own thing, to be indifferent. Isaiah 53:6 says, *"All of us like sheep have gone astray, each of us has turned to his own way."* That is the heart of sin, and that is what you must admit in coming to Christ—that whether you have committed certain sins outwardly or not, inwardly you have gone astray; you have done whatever you wanted to do in disregard to Scripture's commands.

Secondly, in Romans 3:13-14 he goes on to say, *"Their throat is an open grave, with their tongues they keep deceiving, the poison of Asps is under their lips; whose mouth is full of cursing and bitterness."* Not only do we see that at our core we wish to do whatever we want to do regardless of what God says, but now we see that we grieve over the words we speak. He says our throats are like foul, open graves spewing out words of deceit and bitter curses. Yes, we say things that hurt others; we say horrible things to one another: we sin by our words because our hearts are sinful.

He goes on in Romans 3:15-18, *"Their feet are swift to shed blood, destruction and misery are in their paths, and the path of peace they have not known. There is no fear of God before their eyes."* In our very essence and disposition we're sinful; first, in the words that we say to others we reveal our sinful hearts, and second, in our deeds which are deeds of hatred rather than peace. We are not by nature peacemakers; by nature, we are hateful, malicious people who, if given the opportunity to both do it and get away with it, we would kill one another.

Paul says that is true of all of us; but the question is do you think it's true of you? That is the issue. It is true of you, but do you think it is true of you? Do you mourn and lament over these sins, even if you are a believer? This is what we struggle with. Do you confess your sins to God and repent of them? Or do you just figure that everybody else is in the same boat and assume, "I'm okay. He's okay. She's okay. We all behave like this, so what's the big deal?" The big deal is that citizens of the kingdom grieve deeply over their sins because these sins offend their King: that is the bottom line. It does not matter who else does it; if we do it, it should bother us; and if you are a believer, it should bother you.

However, although we enter the kingdom mourning over our sins, the truth is that once we are in the kingdom, we continue to grieve over our sins. New believers need to understand that you never stop grieving. Because when you are a new believer you often don't understand that truth, so you wonder, "Why am I so burdened with my sin? Why is it that as I grow closer to the Lord, I keep seeing my sin?" That is normal; that is the way it is supposed to be. We never stop grieving over our sin regardless of how much we grow in the Lord. In fact, that is one of the great paradoxes of the Christian life—the more mature you are in Christ, the more your sin bothers you. Why? It is because your love for the Lord is so much deeper than at your initial conversion, so it ought to continue bothering you. You love the Lord so much more than you did when you initially became a Christian that your sin against Him is so more grievous to you. That is the way it works.

That ought to be a great encouragement. This is the war that Paul says in Romans 7 goes on in our members. Paul, writing as a mature believer in the most magnificent of all the New Testament letters, opens his heart and is very vulnerable, crying out that he is a wretched sinner. I affirm that Romans 7:14-17 is not about Paul's pre-conversion days. Look at what Paul says: *"For we know that the Law is spiritual, but I am of flesh, sold into bondage to sin."* He is establishing the fact that there is no problem with the Law, the problem is with him. Verses 15-16: *"For what I am doing, I do not understand; for I am not practicing what I would like to do, but I am doing the very thing I hate. But if I do the very thing I do not want to do, I agree with the Law, confessing that the Law is good."* And then he says in verse 17: *"So now, no longer am I the one doing it, but sin which dwells in me."* Paul is admitting that even as a mature believer, when he looks at his life he just sees sin. It does not mean that Paul didn't obey God or that he was backslidden. It just meant that Paul was so godly and so spiritual that any sin grieved him deeply. That is the way it ought to be for all of us.

He says in verse 18, *"For I know that nothing good dwells in me, that is, in my flesh; for the willing is present in me, but the doing of the good is not."* That is one of the reasons why we know Paul is speaking as a believer. No unbeliever in his innermost being wills to do what is right. The human heart is hostile towards God, but here Paul says in Romans 3:19-22, "I want to do what's right, but I don't seem to be able to do that consistently." *"For the good that I want, I do not do, but I practice the very evil that I do not want. But if I am doing the very thing I do not want, I am no longer the one doing it, but sin which dwells in me. I find then the principle that evil is present in me, the one who wants to do good. For I joyfully concur with the law of God in the inner man."* This is Paul, the great apostle, speaking, and once again, he gives us another mark of a true believer: he agrees with the law of God in the inner man. Paul says, "I agree with it. That's my desire; it's what I want to do consistently." In Romans 7:23-25 he states, *"but I see a different law in the members of my body, waging war against the law of my mind and making me a prisoner of the law of sin which is in my members. Wretched man that I am! Who will set me free from the body of this death? Thanks be to God through Jesus Christ our Lord! So then, on the one hand I myself with my mind am serving the law of God, but on the other, with my flesh the law of sin."* Here is the great apostle Paul calling himself a wretched man, crying out for deliverance, and this is not the unique experience of a great apostle. This is true of all genuine believers. Paul was speaking experientially as a believer, not as an apostle. The history of God's people verifies that even the godliest of His people mourn and sorrow over their personal sin.

If you are not familiar with David Brainard, you should be. David Brainard was an 18th century missionary to the

American Indians, a godly man who impacted many lives. In fact, he had a great impact on the life of Jonathan Edwards, a man known as America's greatest theologian. He only lived to be 29 years of age and died serving the Lord as a missionary. He is noted, even to this day, as a great missionary and is renowned for his personal godliness and deep spiritual sensitivity. Here is what David Brainerd recorded in his journal on October 18, 1740: "In my morning devotions, my soul was exceedingly melted, and bitterly mourned over my exceeding sinfulness and vileness."[2] On May 17, 1747, Brainerd wrote this: "At this time God gave me some affecting sense of my own vileness and the exceeding sinfulness of my heart that there seemed to be nothing but sin and corruption within me."[3] This is a man who is grieved over his sin.

The great English preacher, Charles Spurgeon, known as "the Prince of Preachers," said this about himself in one of his sermons in the year 1889:

> Brethren, when I have considered and inwardly perceived the holiness of God's Law, I have felt as though the deep edge of a saber had been drawn across my heart and I have shivered and trembled. What poor creatures we are! The best of men are men at best, and apart from the work of the Holy Spirit and the power of divine grace hell itself does not contain greater monsters than you and I might become.[4]

Those are strong and accurate words! That which the apostle Paul, Brainerd and Spurgeon believed of themselves is also true of us. Perhaps we can't articulate it like they did, but the truth is the same. All Christians feel this way about themselves; they despise the wickedness they see in their hearts and lives and then long and groan to be free of it. That's why Paul said in 2 Corinthians 5:2 that he groaned;

he didn't want to stay in this world battling not only people, but battling with himself and Satan—he wanted to be gone from here.

If you ever get comfortable with your sin to the point that you don't mourn, then something is very wrong. Either you have never truly been converted or else you are a backslidden believer who is too absorbed with yourself to even notice that you are grieving the Holy Spirit by your behavior. You are so caught up in yourself that you don't even know that you are grieving Him. Never be discouraged as a believer, especially if you are new in the faith, by your inward struggle with sin. The struggle is right; the war continues. It is when you don't struggle that you ought to be concerned. It is when you give in that you should be concerned. All true citizens of the kingdom have this inward struggle. It is normal for believers to be continuously bothered by their sin, even as they are growing in the Lord. That is why Jesus said, *"Blessed are those who mourn."* It is not a negative thing; rather, it is a positive thing.

But there is something else to consider. When Jesus said, *"Blessed are those who mourn,"* He certainly intended that our mourning would include not only the sins of others, but also our own sins. We would be wrong to say, "He just meant that we are to mourn over our own sin." That is true, but it goes beyond that. Not only is the faithful child of God grieved over his own personal sinfulness, but it grieves him to see the wasted lives of those who sin against the God he loves. In Psalm 119:136 David said, *"My eyes shed streams of water, because they do not keep Your law."* He looked at his own people and others not obeying the Law and said, "I weep over it." That is what it means to have your heart broken over the sinfulness of others. That is what ought to exist in our own lives as well.

Paul rebuked the church at Corinth because when there was immorality going on there, they were not mourning over that sin, but were proud of their spirit of tolerance. In effect Paul said, "Tolerance? You ought to be mourning at what this man has done! You should mourn him as you discipline him." And as Paul explained his heartache to the Corinthians over their sin, he said in 2 Corinthians 2:4, *"I wrote to you with many tears."* It has been suggested that there were literally tear stains on the original manuscript of Paul's letter because of his grief over their sinful behavior.

Old Testament prophet Jeremiah was known as the "weeping prophet" because he lamented deeply over the sins of his people Israel. Mourning for others certainly characterized the Lord Himself. It is very interesting that there is no record in Scripture that Jesus ever laughed. I am not saying that He didn't laugh, just that there is no record that He ever laughed. I realize that is an argument from silence but that is a pretty loud statement. There are many statements that He mourned and wept and grieved. He is known as *"a man of sorrows and acquainted with grief"* (Isaiah 53:3) and His grief was not over His own sin, because He had none.

So what was the source of His grief? It was grief over us. Remember how He wept over Jerusalem because of their rejection of Him? On another occasion His heart was so broken over the damaging effect that sin had upon people at the grave of His friend Lazarus that the Bible gives us the briefest verse in all of Scripture. John 11:35 says, *"Jesus wept."* Why was He weeping? It could not be because of Lazarus' death because in just a few moments He was going to raise Lazarus back to life; so that explanation wouldn't make sense. I believe He was grieving and weeping because He saw the heartache that comes from sin's impact on people as He saw the mourners all around Him. He saw the sadness and it pained His heart, and He saw the damaging effects of sin, and so the Scripture says He wept.

That should be our response to the sin that is all around us as well. When you and I read or see the atrocities that go on in our world, or observe it in the lives of friends and relatives and others we know, it should evoke not only feelings of disgust but it should also evoke feelings of mourning and grief.

Here's how D. Martyn Lloyd-Jones explained how the true Christian should react to the sin in others that he sees all around him. He wrote,

> He must mourn because of the very nature of sin itself because it has ever entered into the world and has led to these terrible results. Indeed he mourns because he has some understanding of what sin means to God, of God's utter abhorrence and hatred of it. This terrible thing that would stab, as it were, into the very heart of God if it could, this rebelliousness and arrogance of man, the results of listening to Satan—it grieves Him and He mourns because of it.[5]

So I say to you, be careful about growing callous to the sins of others. It is so easy to do that because we're so familiar with the sins of others in our sin saturated world. Be careful that you don't become uncaring and indifferent because you are so familiar. Any sin in any form committed by anyone should grieve us, and if it doesn't it simply means that if you're a believer, you need a fresh glimpse of God's holiness. It ought to break your heart; it should not just be news to you; it ought to be a grievous thing to hear of sin.

Now, with all this emphasis that we've seen in Scripture concerning mourning, are we then to conclude that citizens of the kingdom are depressed people? I think that's a logical question. Are we to walk about downcast and sullen about our many sins? The answer to that is emphatically "No!" No, because Jesus concluded this Beatitude with a precious promise that keeps us from being morose, keeps us from being miserable over our sins. Not only did He say, *"Blessed are those who mourn over their sin,"* but He said, *"Blessed are those who mourn for they shall be"*—what? They shall be *"comforted"*!

So let's examine that phrase: what did Jesus mean by "comforted"? Being comforted is the specific result of being blessed. You see, the blessing is not in mourning itself as there's no virtue or blessing in mourning; that's not where the blessing is. The blessing is in the truth that God comforts those who mourn over sin; that's the blessing, and it's this wonderful comfort that keeps us from being morbid and gloomy people.

Allow me to explain and put this together for us. First, we need to discover what Jesus specifically meant about this comfort. In what way will those who mourn be comforted? The comfort that He's referring to is a present comfort. It's not something you get at the end of life when you die. It's not something reserved for a far, distant, prophetic, future event; no, that's not what He's referring to. When Jesus said, *"Blessed are those who mourn for they shall be comforted,"* the *"shall be"* doesn't refer to something that's in the distant future; rather the thought here is that the comfort comes right after the mourning. That's why it's presented *"shall be"*— it's immediate! In other words, *"Blessed are those who mourn for they* immediately *will be comforted."*

So what kind of present comfort is Jesus talking about? The only comfort that can relieve the stress of a guilt-ridden individual is the comfort that comes from being forgiven of our sins. In Christ, they are forgiven—completely forgiven. All sins—past, present and future—are judicially wiped out. The Bible says in Hebrews 8:12, *"I will remember their sins no more."* That doesn't mean that God forgets. He doesn't have amnesia. However, it does mean that He *"will remember them no more"* in the sense that He chooses, in mercy and grace because of Christ's atoning work and because His holiness has been satisfied, to no longer hold sin against us. That's exactly what it means, which is why David, in Psalm 32:1-2, said *"How blessed is he whose transgression is forgiven, whose sin is covered. How blessed is the man to whom the Lord does not impute iniquity, and in whose spirit there is no deceit."* David said it's a blessed thing, a comforting thing, to be forgiven; which is exactly what Jesus means here.

Here's how it works—when you come under deep conviction of sin as the Lord is working in your heart bringing you to salvation, you come under deep conviction of sin because the Lord has opened your eyes. He's opened your hearts to see how utterly depraved you really are, and you also see how holy and just He is. You see that first because you can't see your sinfulness unless you see His holiness. You see that He's holy; you see that He's just. But in seeing His perfection, you see how far short you have fallen of that glory. You see that you're a wicked sinner, with no hope of ever pleasing God with your own merit. And so you're devastated because not only do you realize you deserve eternal judgment but you realize what a wicked individual you really are, and so you mourn. You're disgusted with your behavior, you're disgusted with your attitude, you're disgusted with your sinfulness. But as you mourn over your many sins (and I don't believe God initially shows us all of our sin or we would die of a heart attack right on the spot), you see another side of God. You've already seen His holiness and justice and righteousness, but now you begin to see that He's not only holy and just; but He's also merciful, loving, compassionate, and gracious. And, in His mercy, He actually became a man; He became a man in the person of Jesus Christ; and Jesus Christ, in dying for sinners, satisfied His own demands for justice. He was the satisfaction! The Bible's big theological word for that is "propitiation." He satisfied the holiness of God by His own punishment, or being punished in our place.

Therefore, when the Lord draws us to Himself to save our souls, we come to Him as guilt-ridden, broken, grieving sinners mourning over the great wickedness we see in our lives. But in turning to Him for salvation from these many sins, we experience the incredible comfort that comes through forgiveness. It's a paradox; we're mourning but we're comforted in our mourning because we understand that there is complete forgiveness—not partial, but complete forgiveness, based on the atoning work of Christ and that alone. Those who mourn are those who are comforted and we're the only ones who can experience this comfort. You must mourn before you are comforted. We're the only ones because we're the only ones who experienced God's saving forgiveness.

That's the prophetic message of Isaiah 61 to which Jesus referred in Luke 4:18-21, when He stood up in the synagogue in Nazareth, read from Isaiah, and then said, *"Today this Scripture has been fulfilled in your hearing."* Isaiah 61:1 referred to the Messiah as the One who will *"bind up the brokenhearted."* He said He will comfort all who mourn.

Luke 2:25 tells us that Simeon was a devout man who was present when Mary and Joseph brought the infant Jesus into the temple, and Simeon was looking for *"the consolation of Israel,"* and when he saw Jesus he rejoiced because He was that consolation. He is the consolation of Israel and He's the consolation of everyone who comes to Him for salvation. That's why at the end of Matthew 11:28 Jesus said, *"Come to Me all you who are weary and heavy laden and I will give you rest"*. He means heavy laden with sin; weary with sin. He wasn't talking about physically being tired, though that might come with it, but He was talking about being *heavy laden,* burdened with your sin. He said in Matthew 11:29 *"Take my yoke upon you and learn from Me, for I am gentle and humble in heart and you'll find rest for your souls."* That's the comfort, the blessed comfort.

But this comfort is not limited to our salvation experience alone. It too, is part of the ongoing Christian life because every time we sin, we are driven (we ought to be driven) to the Lord to confess our sin, and as we confess our sin, He continues to forgive us. It's not the initial, judicial forgiveness of salvation that covers everything for eternity. But rather, this is the daily cleansing; this is the fellowship forgiveness. This is the restoration of joy in our lives. The moment we turn to Him in repentance, He cleanses us and He returns the peace and the joy that we forfeit when we sin. That's how it works. That's the blessed comfort of the Christian today. And in the future, you know what happens? You'll experience this comfort in its fullness. You'll experience it in its fullness because there won't be any more personal sin to grieve over, and that is what the Bible is referring to when it says, *"At that time He will wipe away every tear from their eyes. There will no longer be any death. There'll no longer be any mourning or crying or pain"* (Revelation 21:4). At the end of time, in the eternal state, we'll know the fullness of this comfort that we taste today. But until that time arrives, we continue to mourn over our sin and, at the same time, we continue to be comforted—comforted by His ongoing forgiveness. That's the balance between grief and comfort that keeps us from becoming gloomy, depressed people.

I read of a woman who lived in the Puritan era, who on her wedding day, refused to wear a white dress. She was dressed all in black because she just felt that her Christian faith was no laughing matter. I don't know what her husband thought about it, but that's a distortion of what the Bible teaches. The citizens of the kingdom, in spite of their continual, eternal grief are not miserable people; we're not like that. Although we weep over our sins, it is something which is internal that others don't see. We don't want to put on a show; that would be like fasting and letting everybody know about it. "Oh, I'm weeping over my sins. Don't you?" That's pseudo-spirituality and that's not what the Bible is talking about. It's internal—you know it and God knows it, but others don't need to know it. Yet at the same time that we are weeping over our sins internally, we are rejoicing because of God's grace and mercy, and others ought to know about that. Remember, if you have the joy of the Lord in your heart, notify your face. You see, it's this paradoxical perspective that gives us a warmth and affection that makes us attractive to unbelievers. Nobody is attracted to someone's who's gloomy; no one wants to be around people like that—not even believers want to be around other believers like that, let alone unbelievers.

There ought to be joy that characterizes your life, not misery. But without God's comfort and God's forgiveness there is misery. You may laugh now but in the future you'll mourn and weep as there is no comfort apart from the forgiveness found in Christ. If you die before turning to Christ for salvation, you will only experience eternal torment because God is holy. He will not make an exception and say, "Well now, you're such a nice person, come on in!" It doesn't work that way. You're not a nice person, I'm not a nice person, no one is a nice person in our hearts, and God knows that, which means there is no hope for any comfort outside of Christ. And so I urge you, if you've never become a true Christian by repenting and trusting Christ to save you, then do so immediately. Admit your sinful rebellion towards Him and you will experience not only mourning over your sin but comfort and forgiveness as well.

If you are already a citizen of His kingdom, then you need to make sure that there is nothing hindering you from mourning over your sin. There are several things you can do that will keep you from having hindrances to mourning. First, have a clear view of God's character. When you study the Bible, do not look just for promises for yourself but also look to understand God's nature and His attributes—His righteousness, holiness, love, mercy, power, and sovereignty. By understanding God's qualities, you will see your sins against the backdrop of His holiness and you will mourn over it. Therefore I encourage you to read books that examine God's character.

Second, have a clear view of yourself. Some people don't have a clear view of themselves and they live in self-deceit. How do you get a clear view of yourself? I would suggest taking time during the day, or perhaps at the end of the day (as the ancients used to do) and look back to reflect upon your activities, your attitudes, your behavior for that day. How have you spoken to others today? Kindly? Sharply? What has been your attitude throughout the day? Impatient or patient? Have you harbored any ill thoughts towards anyone even if they don't know about it? Have you done something you shouldn't have? Have you not done something you should have? God knows the truth, so be honest in your daily self-assessment. By taking the time to run over these things in your mind, you will become aware of your sins and you will grieve. So, you don't ever want to become so busy with activities, even activities in the Lord's service, that you don't have time to examine yourself for any sin that needs to be addressed. And how do you address sin? You address it by mourning, by confessing, and by experiencing His marvelous comfort that comes through forgiveness.

In conclusion, get a clear glimpse of God and a clear glimpse of your sin, and you'll be broken. God loves a broken, contrite heart before Him. The world doesn't love brokenness and contriteness; rather, they despise it because it throws a wet blanket on their party. But citizens of the kingdom are different from the world. You follow the King who was a weeper and knew what it was to lament.

In Matthew 16:13 Jesus said, *"Who do men say that I am?"* Someone said to Him, *"Some say you're Jeremiah the prophet."* Now why would they say that? They said it probably because He wept like Jeremiah. The weeping was so characteristic of His life that it reminded them of the weeping prophet and they thought, "He's come back." You need to weep over your sin. Are you broken? Get a clear glimpse of who God is and then get a clear glimpse of who you are and you will weep and be broken over your sin.

How about the sins of others? Have you grown, as I find my own heart, calloused to the news? Have you become indifferent and familiar with it in such a way that it doesn't seem to penetrate? This is where we need to ask the Lord to break us in a real genuine way. Have you been rejoicing in God's forgiveness? Forgiveness is not something you feel rather it's something you take by faith. If you're in Christ, then thank God for His forgiveness. And don't buy into the modern psychological term where you have to forgive yourself. The Bible doesn't teach that. You didn't sin against you—you sinned against God. You need to thank God for His forgiveness whether you feel like you're forgiven or not. If you're in Christ, you're forgiven; otherwise we make God a liar and that's not true. Let's bow together in prayer...

> *Oh, Father, thank You for Your Word...such a penetrating, paradox of a Beatitude. But Lord I pray that You will break my heart over my sin and the sins of others. And I pray also that you'll do that with all of our people. I pray especially for those who are outside of the kingdom that they might see their sinfulness and be moved by the Holy Spirit to come to the Savior, and that they would weep over their own sin and experience the joy and the comfort that comes with forgiveness.*

> *Lord, I pray that You will use your Word greatly in our lives, and that we will be different. I pray, Lord, that You will help us to have that balance of not being*

gloomy but internally weeping, and yet being attractive people on the outside; rejoicing and enjoying the peace and the relationship and the forgiveness that we have in You. We pray this in Your precious name, Amen.

---

[1]Lloyd-Jones, D. Martyn.Studies in the Sermon on the Mount. Grand Rapids: Eerdmans Publishing Company, 1959-60. 47.

[2]http://www.jesus.org.uk/vault/library/brainerd_diary.pdf. 15.

[3]Ibid. 150-151.

[4]Spurgeon, Charles.*The Mediator—The Interpreter.*Sermon No. 2097. Metropolitan Tabernacle, Newington. July 28, 1889.

[5]Lloyd-Jones. 48.

Chapter 8

CHRIST OUR ADVOCATE
1 John 2:1-2
September 6, 2009

Misunderstandings can lead to all kinds of problems. They can destroy family relationships. They can create conflicts with individuals that are hard to resolve. They can do irreparable damage in the business world, and they can cause churches to split. That's what misunderstandings can do. They do a lot of detrimental things in our lives, so we all recognize that serious problems can result from poor communication that causes misunderstandings.

Likewise, when we look at the New Testament, we notice that, at times, Bible writers made a point of clarifying certain theological issues they were concerned could be misunderstood. For example, in Romans 6, the apostle Paul realized that for the first five chapters of his letter, he emphasized nothing but grace. He spoke of man being a sinner and man being worthy of eternal damnation, and then he spoke of God's provision for salvation in Christ. Then at the end of chapters three, four, and five, he emphasizes the grace of God in Christ. But when he comes to chapter six, Paul, under the inspiration of the Spirit of God, recognizes that he might be misunderstood. There might be some misunderstanding by some in the church at Rome that this might be an encouragement to sin or a license to sin. So he says in Romans 6:1-2, *"What shall we say then..."* He's saying, "What shall we say then in light of all this grace? *"Are we to continue in sin so that grace may increase?"* He knows that's what some are thinking. He then says, *"May it never be! How shall we who died to sin still live in it?"* Paul deliberately pauses in his letter to make sure that he is not misunderstood.

A little bit later, he does the same thing, though not in quite the same dramatic fashion. In Romans chapters 9-11, he clarifies some issues about God's plan for Israel. Why? Because he realizes that there were some in the church who might misunderstand God's grace in saving so many Gentiles. They might conclude that now that there are so many Gentiles in the church, God must have set Israel aside permanently because of her rejection of Jesus as the Messiah. And so Romans 9, 10 and 11 are written to clarify and to make sure that there's no misunderstanding that God has not cast Israel aside permanently. There is a plan for Israel. God is faithful to His chosen people.

In 1 John 2:1-2 the apostle John addresses an important issue that he also wants to make sure is not a misunderstanding. He writes, *"My little children, I am writing these things to you so that you may not sin. And if anyone sins, we have an Advocate with the Father, Jesus Christ the righteous; and He Himself is the propitiation for our sins; and not for ours only, but also for those of the whole world."*

At the beginning of verse one, John immediately states the matter he does not want misunderstood. He writes, *"My little children, I'm writing these things to you so that you may not sin."* Writing with the heart of a loving, tender pastor, as an older, spiritually mature father to them, John addresses his readers as *"little children."* This doesn't mean that these Christians were spiritually immature or that they were all relatively new in the faith. The term *"little children"* is actually used seven times in 1 John. It's an expression of endearment, and an expression of tender affection. We know that on at least one occasion, and we can assume that it happened many times, the apostle John had heard the Master, the Lord Jesus Himself, speak these very same words when addressing the apostles. In John 13:33, in the Upper Room giving His farewell discourse, Jesus said, *"Little children, I am with you a little while longer,"* and now many years later, as an old man and the last living apostle, John embraces this expression *"little children,"* and he uses it to speak to his precious flock.

And so it is that with his spiritual children, those under his nurturing care, he wants to make sure there is no misunderstanding about what he has written concerning sin. He wants them to know that what he has written about sin in what we call 1 John 1:8-9; specifically the fact that as believers in Christ we still sin and confess our sins and receive God's cleansing forgiveness, should never be taken as an encouragement to sin. On the contrary, he tells them that he is writing to them so that they would not sin. In other words, even though we still sin and God is *"faithful and righteous to forgive us our sins"* (1 John 1:9), that shouldn't be misunderstood as a license or an encouragement in any way to go ahead and sin. Remember, John also wrote in the first chapter that *"God is light and in Him there is no darkness"* (1 John 1:5), meaning that God's character is perfect. There is no sin; there is no defect in Him. That truth about God's perfect character should make each of us realize that because sin is so hideous and so revolting in God's sight that, even though we do still sin and He's gracious to forgive us, we shouldn't sin.

That is a heavy thought to consider and one which we often don't consider, because as believers in Christ we still struggle with sin. We have many sin issues in our lives—

pride, lust, jealousy, covetousness, words that we say, attitudes we display, and many other things. We sin! We struggle with sin, and confession is the normal part of every single believer's life, so it's hard for us to grasp that God's will, as revealed here, is that we don't sin. That is God's desire, and we must not lower the standard. That is precisely what the apostle John is saying: *"I am writing these things to you so that you may not sin."* Is this even possible? Yes, of course it is or otherwise Scripture wouldn't say it. The Bible never commands us as believers to do something that we are incapable of doing. This is a command and it is God's standard. Is it possible? Yes.

Let's step back for a moment. Before coming to faith in Christ, Scripture says that we were *"slaves to sin"* (Romans 6:6, 20). We were enslaved to sin. We couldn't do anything but sin. We made choices in the realm of sin because we had a sin nature. You will only follow the dictates of your nature, and if you have a sin nature, the natural bent of your heart is to sin. We could do nothing else, and the most significant passage of Scripture that reveals this is Ephesians 2:1-3. It says, *"And you were dead in your trespasses and sins..."* You had no life in you, spiritually speaking. You had physical life but not spiritual life. You were dead; dead to God and dead to any responsiveness towards the Spirit of God. You were dead in your sins *"...in which you formerly walked according to the course of this world, according to the prince of the power of the air, of the spirit that is now working in the sons of disobedience."* He's saying, "You were like everybody else; living, but only physically." *"Among them, too, we all formerly lived..."* This is how we lived...totally *"in the lust of our flesh, indulging the desires of the flesh and of the mind, and were by nature children of wrath, even as the rest."* That was our nature. We were children of wrath. We hated God. We did whatever we wanted, and our lives were total sin. There was a bondage to our sin nature.

However, at regeneration something wonderful happened. We received a brand new nature. Peter calls it a *"divine nature"* (2 Peter 1:4).Therefore, we were set free from being slaves to sin, and because of this new nature, we, as believers, have the power to say "no" to sin. We are not enslaved to sin like before. Something wonderful has happened to us. That doesn't mean that we don't sin. It just means that we don't *have* to sin now. Paul addresses this in Romans 6:17-18. He says, *"But thanks be to God that though you were slaves of sin, you became obedient from the heart to that form of teaching to which you were committed."* In other words, you became obedient to the Gospel. You became obedient to the truth of the Word of God, and having been freed from sin, you became slaves of righteousness. We don't have to sin anymore. If we sin, we choose to sin, knowing full well what we're doing. Although we continue to struggle with sin in our lives, ultimately it is the desire of every true believer to be free of sin. We don't want to sin. We struggle with it, but we really don't want to sin. We long to be free from the bondage and the sins of this world.

Listen to the wise and biblically balanced words of Joel Beeke from his commentary on 1 John as he addresses this very issue. He writes,

> The true believer aims high, John says. His goal is not to sin at all. No doubt you've heard the expression "Aim at nothing and you'll hit it every time." Likewise, if you aim at something less than perfection, you will certainly achieve it. You might object saying, "Yes, but if I aim at perfection, I will not achieve that either. Why try reaching for a goal that I know I cannot accomplish? A goal should be achievable."

> If you do not firmly determine to break with sin, you will have little success in overcoming sin in your life. Sin should be abhorrent to you. You will not reach perfection this side of eternity, of course. As long as we are in the body, we sin. We grieve God and one another with our sin, but one of the great marks of a genuine Christian is that once the seed of new life is planted within him, he has a new attitude to sin. He beings to see sin for what it is, viewing it as so heinous that it nailed the Son of God to a cross and moved God to abandon His Son. The believer longs to be free of sin so that he might love God purely for who He is and what He has done.[1]

That is a brilliant statement because it recognizes that, yes, we struggle with sin but we don't give into it saying, "Well, what else can I do? I may as well aim low." No, we don't aim low; we aim high.

This is precisely the message of the New Testament. Not only has God justified us in Christ, our Salvation, but He continues to sanctify us day by day, moment by moment, so that we will be more and more conformed to the very image of His Son. That's the message of Romans 8:28- 29. Paul writes, *"We know that God causes all things to work together for good to those who love God."* That's us! Everything that happens in our lives is sent by God for our good. In what sense? He says, *"to those who are called according to His purpose,"* so the question is, what is His purpose in our lives? Why is everything working together for good? The next verse says, *"for those whom He foreknew, He also predestined"*—this is His ultimate purpose—*"to become conformed to the image of His Son, so that He would be the firstborn among many brethren."* That is to say, God's ultimate purpose for you and for me is to conform us perfectly to Christ's character. We know that someday that will take place ultimately when we enter His presence, but it starts right now. It starts the moment you're saved. The process begins at salvation.

Now there is a paradox in all of this. As we grow in Christ and get closer to the Lord in our spiritual walk with Him, we sin less. We really do, but it doesn't seem to be the case because we see our sin much more clearly. We hate our sin more, so the closer we get to the Lord, the more we see our sin. We hate our sin so much more than we ever did before. And we are sinning less, but it just doesn't seem like that. It seems like we're sinning more, but actually we aren't. This is precisely why we cry out with the apostle Paul, *"Wretched man that I am! Who will set me free from the body of this death?"* (Romans 7:24). You may never have articulated those exact words, but that ought to be the heart cry of your life if you're a believer. You call yourself a wretched man. "Who will deliver me? I don't want to sin anymore. Lord, I want to be free of this sin." So we sin, but we hate it. We long for deliverance and that great day when we stand before the Lord without any sin.

So what are we going to do about this predicament? John tells us that He who is Light does not want us to sin, not even once, and we dare not lower the standard by saying, "Well, there's nothing I can do about it." No, this is God's Word. Even though we know that we do sin, we struggle not to sin. The good news is that God knows our frailty and He knows how weak we are. He knows how susceptible we are to sin and to Satan's temptations, and so He's made a perfect provision for us when we do sin. That's why the apostle John proceeds to state in the very next phrase of verse 1, *"and if anyone sins."* This is not to be taken as an encouragement to sin. It simply means that even though Scripture commands us not to sin, if a believer should sin—and the thought is that God knows that we do and will sin—then what happens?

Let me explain what should not happen, but so often does. When believers sin, especially if we sin in an area with which we continuously struggle and we're defeated by it, we can become very disheartened and very discouraged in our own walk. At times we may even fall into despair when overcome by sin. Sometimes we even begin to doubt our salvation and become susceptible to those wicked thoughts that come from the enemy, such as, "How can you be a Christian and do something like this? You did this yesterday, you did it today, and you know you're going to do it tomorrow. Just give up. You're not a Christian." That's tough. It's at times like this that we have great difficulty recognizing God's forgiveness. We often confess our sin over and over and over again and beat ourselves up emotionally and spiritually.

The good news is that you don't have to be in despair. You don't have to be discouraged. You don't have to receive the devil's doubts, and you don't have to beat yourself up emotionally or spiritually. We know that is true because the apostle John proceeds to address that very concern by telling us that God has made perfect provision for when we sin. First, he tells us that Jesus Christ is our advocate with the Father. Then, second, he tells us that Jesus Christ is the propitiation for our sin.

The first truth about Jesus Christ, through whom God has made provision for us when we sin, is that Christ is our advocate with the Father. First John 2:1 says, *"And if anyone sins, we have an Advocate with God the Father, Jesus Christ the righteous."* What an amazing truth! The word translated *Advocate* literally means "called alongside of." It speaks of someone who is summoned to the assistance of another. In ancient times, this word was often used in legal settings in reference to a lawyer who came to the defense of his client. I recall being in the city of Rome and seeing the word "Advocate" on the outside of a building, and I asked a friend who grew up in Italy where his parents were missionaries,

"Does that mean he's a lawyer?" He told me, "That's exactly what it means." So that word is used in today's world, just as it was in the ancient world, to speak of a defense attorney.

Interestingly, the word in the Greek text which John uses here is also found in the Gospel of John, the only other place in the New Testament that uses this word. John quotes Jesus using this word as a title for the Holy Spirit. It's often translated "Comforter," but it's the same word that means "one called alongside to help." However, in 1 John, this is the only time in the Bible where this word is used to speak strictly of Jesus Christ. He's not speaking about the Holy Spirit here. He calls Jesus Christ our *"Advocate with the Father."*

What does this mean? It means that right now—at this very moment—Jesus Christ, our defense attorney, is in heaven before the Father pleading our case. In fact, the Greek word that is translated *"with,"* as in *"with the Father,"* has the root meaning of "face to face." That is to say, when we sin, Jesus Christ—our personal Advocate and defense Attorney who is facing God the Father—pleads our case before Him. And what is it that Jesus, who is face to face with the Father, says in our defense when we sin? I'll tell you what He doesn't say. He doesn't say, "Do you know what, Father? That person sinned but he didn't mean it." That wouldn't be true. We sin, and we mean it. We can't make excuses like, "Well, I didn't mean it." We definitely mean it when we sin. He certainly doesn't say, "It's true that person sinned, Father, but he's really not responsible for what he did. There were extenuating circumstances. If You could only see the background that he or she came out of, you'd understand," as if God doesn't know our background. No, He doesn't say that because that wouldn't be true either. We sin because we choose to sin. It's not our father's fault or our mother's fault. It's our fault. There are no extenuating circumstances that make us sin. Christ also doesn't say,

"Well, she doesn't know what she's doing." She certainly does know what she's doing.

So how does the Lord plead our case? He shows the Father His pierced hands, His pierced feet, His wounded side, and He says, "Father, it's true. They've sinned, but I have paid the price for their sin with my life. I have suffered on the Cross for them, and Your wrath and judgment were poured out on Me in their place." That's what He says! That's our defense!

Whether or not Jesus actually says those words or words to that effect, no one can say with certainty, but regardless of whether or not He utters actual words in our defense, the fact is that He stands in the presence of God the Father pleading our case. He doesn't deny that we've sinned. He says, "That is a sin, but I paid for that sin and my pierced hands and side and feet prove it." And note this: His defense is always correct. He is never, nor will He ever, lose a case. That's why John refers to our Advocate as *"Jesus Christ the righteous."* That's not just randomly thrown into the text; that's John's point. In other words, He's perfectly righteous in our defense. In the words of one writer, "He never resorts to anything crooked to get His clients off the hook."[2] He never lies about our sin; He speaks the truth to the Father about not only our sin but also Himself. He has paid for every sin we have ever done, every sin we might do now, and every sin we will do in the future. That's the case. He's our Advocate. So, when you feel condemned as a believer, understand you don't need to give in to your feelings. You are to confess your sin to God, as 1 John 1:8-9 tells us, and then believe what God says. Your Advocate, the righteous Christ, is in heaven right now pleading your case before the Father. And He has won the case. You are forgiven.

It was Charles Spurgeon who expressed this so well when he spoke of his own experience when he sinned. Listen to what Spurgeon said, "Sinner as I am, and never more consciously so than I am now that God's Spirit has enlightened me, I still know that if any man sins, we have an Advocate with the Father. And I, black, foul, and filthy; more foul and filthy than I ever thought myself to be, put my case into the hand of my Advocate, and leave it there forever."[3] That's the way to have victory. That's what we need to do. We need to confess our sins, believe that our Advocate has pled and won our case, and leave it there. You don't have to torment yourself.

There's a song we like to sing at our church that puts this concept of Christ's advocacy into precious words. Think about the truth in these words:

Before the throne of God above
I have a strong and perfect plea.
A great high Priest whose Name is Love
Who ever lives and pleads for me.

My name is graven on His hands,
My name is written on His heart.
I know that while in Heaven He stands
No tongue can bid me thence depart.

When Satan tempts me to despair
And tells me of the guilt within,
Upward I look and see Him there
Who made an end of all my sin.[4]

That's glorious, biblical worship! That's the place of victory.

So the first provision that God has made for us when we sin is that Jesus Christ is our righteous Advocate. But the question is: How can this be? How can Jesus defend us before the Father when we have sinned and transgressed God's laws so many times and continue to do it? John proceeds to explain how Jesus Christ can be our Advocate before a holy God by giving us a second truth about Christ and God's provision for when we sin.

Not only is Jesus Christ the Advocate, He is also the propitiation for our sins. Verse two says, *"And He Himself is the propitiation for our sins."* What does this mean? The word *propitiation* is a big theological word but it's not a difficult word to grasp. It means to "appease or to satisfy someone's wrath." Just think of satisfaction or appeasement. The Bible presents God as angry and offended by our sins, and His holiness and justice demand that the price for sin be paid by pouring out His righteous wrath upon those who have sinned. That's exactly what God did, but He didn't pour it out upon us. We had a substitute—His own Son, Jesus Christ. When Jesus died, He became the propitiation for our sins, because the Father poured out His wrath upon Him, and, as one theologian put it, "it quenched the terrible fire of His burning anger."[5] Christ's death satisfied the wrath of God for our sins. In other words, in the death of Jesus Christ, God's holiness and justice was propitiated. There's no lack of satisfaction. It was completely satisfied. He is a righteous judge, and His perfect justice was satisfied by the payment for our sin by our substitute, His own perfect Son. That's why Jesus can be our Advocate with the Father. Only He can make the case that we are no longer condemned because He Himself has satisfied the fury and the wrath of God's anger by dying in our place and, thus, has perfectly satisfied the justice of God. That's why we can sing that great hymn, *The Solid Rock*, which says, "My hope is built on nothing less than Jesus' blood and righteousness."[6]

This is why salvation is solely by grace. It can't be any other way. You can't merit salvation. Christ has paid it all, and God is completely satisfied with that payment. It is finished. The incredible truth about propitiation is that God took the initiative. We didn't. We didn't care. We wouldn't do anything about this. We would just go on hating God. But even though we were the ones who sinned against Him and wanted nothing to do with Him, He came after us. Notice 1 John 4:10. This is the only other time this word *propitiation* is used in 1 John. *"In this is love, not that we loved God, but that He loved us and sent his Son to be the propitiation for our sins."* What an amazing truth! His love—not anything in us, but His love—is what moved Him to send Christ to be the propitiation for our sins.

Notice how John closes this brief section in chapter two. He says, *"And he is the propitiation for our sins, and not for ours only but also for those of the whole world."* Some have interpreted these words to mean that Jesus has paid the sins of every single person who has ever lived in the world. That can't be. If that were the case, every single individual would go to heaven when they die, because it would mean that every sin was paid for. But you say, "But they have to believe." Yes, but it would also mean that the price of their sin of unbelief was paid. It can't be. Otherwise, everybody would go to heaven because the price of all their sins would have been paid. That would be the doctrine of universalism, meaning universally, everyone will be saved. That's not the case. People who don't trust Christ don't go to heaven, they go to hell. Scripture says in Revelation 21:8 that those who continue to reject Christ will have their place in the Lake of Fire that burns forever and ever.

In the Bible, the words "world" or "all" are not always used to refer to every single individual. It's not "all" in the sense of "everyone." For example, Titus 2:11 says, *"For the grace of God has appeared, bringing salvation to all men."* Paul certainly doesn't mean that every person has salvation. It just means people from all walks of humanity – Jewish people, Gentile people, Roman people, Greek people—all people of the earth. It means that salvation has come to all. It's not restricted to Jewish people anymore.

So what does John mean by saying that Christ is the propitiation for the sins of the whole world? He simply means that Christ's death didn't satisfy the wrath of God for only his first century readers or for the small group of people who made up the church in the first century, but it was all those from among fallen humanity, down through the ages, that He would draw to Himself for salvation. That includes us. He's the propitiation, not only for the sins of John's readers, but for us as well.

If you are one of those who has been drawn to Jesus Christ, then understand that God wants you to grow in Him so that you won't sin. Don't settle for anything less. Don't lower the standard. But, since we do sin, we don't have to be defeated. We don't have to be in despair. We don't have to beat ourselves up. We don't have to keep confessing the sin over and over and over again. When you've done it once, move on. Why? Because we have a righteous Advocate who has never lost a case, and He can be our righteous Advocate because He is also the propitiation for our sins. God is satisfied. You can't do anything to undo that or to make Him more satisfied. If God the Father has accepted Christ's payment for your sin, all of your sin is forgiven. As Spurgeon said, "Put [your] case in the hand of [your] Advocate and leave it there."[7]

If you haven't trusted Christ, then come to Him today. Let Him deal with your sinful guilt. Let Him be your Advocate. Let Him be your propitiation. Let's bow for prayer...

Lord, help us to remember these precious truths. Help us to preach the Gospel to ourselves. Thank You that even now, Lord Jesus, You are our Advocate, with pierced hands, pierced feet, and wounded side, standing before the Father pleading our case. Lord, we have nothing more to plead. You are our Defender, and You are our Defense. We have no excuse. We have sinned. We are to blame. So thank You for being our defense attorney who has never lost a case because You died for us.

Father, thank You for being satisfied with the death of Your Son. What a hideous future we would face forever in hell were it not for Christ being the propitiation; were You not satisfied with His death on our behalf. Thank you for that.

Lord, when we sing our worship songs, help us to sing them with meaning, with passion, with worship, with understanding. And, Lord, if we sin tonight or tomorrow, help us to remember what we've studied. Help us, as Spurgeon said, to put our case into the pierced hands of our Advocate and leave it there. May we know the joy in doing that. We pray this all in Jesus' name...Amen.

---

[1] Beeke, Joel.*The Epistles of John.* Darlington, England: Evangelical Press, 2006. 55.

[2] Hiebert, D. Edmond.*The Epistles of John.* Greenville, SC: Bob Jones University Press, 1991. 74.

[3] Spurgeon, Charles.*The Sinner's Advocate.*Sermon No. 515. Metropolitan Tabernacle, Newington. June 21, 1863.

[4] *Before the Throne of God Above.*Lyrics by Charitie Lees Bancroft. 1863.

[5] Beeke, Joel. 52.

[6] *The Solid Rock.*Lyrics by Edward Mote. 1836.

[7] Spurgeon, Charles.*The Sinner's Advocate.*Sermon No. 515. Metropolitan Tabernacle, Newington. June 21, 1863.

Chapter 9

Testing the Spirits
1 John 4:1-3
September 5, 2010

In a book titled *Fool's Gold*, the author points out that in the California gold rush of 1849 many prospectors discovered that not everything that appeared to be gold really was. Riverbeds and rock quarries were filled with golden specks that looked like genuine gold, but in reality, they were just worthless chunks of iron pyrite; therefore, this iron pyrite took on the name "fool's gold." That's where we get that term from, and miners developed certain ways to test or discern if these rocks were real gold or if they were worthless pyrite.

The gold rush of California ended a long time ago, but in the spiritual realm there continues to be a great deal of "fool's gold," because not everything that glitters and sounds good and sounds godly really is. The Bible has a great deal to say to believers about how to discern what is from God and what is from the evil one, Satan. One of the places in Scripture that focuses on this issue of discernment is 1 John 4:1-6. It says:

Beloved, do not believe every spirit, but test the spirits to see whether they are from God, because many false prophets have gone out into the world. By this you know the Spirit of God: every spirit that confesses that Jesus Christ has come in the flesh is from God; and every spirit that does not confess Jesus is not from God; this is the spirit of the antichrist, of which you have heard that it is coming, and now it is already in the world. You are from God, little children, and have overcome them; because greater is He who is in you than he who is in the world. They are from the world; therefore they speak as from the world, and the world listens to them. We are from God; he who knows God listens to us; he who is not from God does not listen to us. By this we know the spirit of truth and the spirit of error.

In these verses, the apostle John shows a great deal of pastoral concern. In fact, he even calls his readers *"beloved."* He knows that they've been impacted by false teachers who have come into their church, negatively influenced them, and then left their assembly. 1 John 2:19 says that the false teachers *"have left their assembly,"* but they left the people hurting. They continued to have an influence upon them even though they were no longer physically there. In fact, this entire letter is written to help these dear Christians who were staggering in their Christian lives, thinking they might not even be saved because these false teachers had said that they (the believers) weren't enlightened like they (the teachers) were. These were Gnostic teachers; therefore, they were not saved. So these people understood about false teachers who had impacted them, and they needed to understand how to discern between the spirit of truth and the spirit of error. How could they know who was a false teacher and who was a true teacher?

But before we examine their situation and the specific passage before us, I think it's important for us to understand that it's not just John's readers who needed to hear this. We also need discernment today. That is one of the great lacking points in the evangelical church. The average Christian is to have discernment to know what is of God and what is not of God, so that we will not be deceived by those who claim to speak from God but do not.

One of the things that has never ceased to amaze me is how Christians can so easily be attracted to teaching that clearly is not based on the Bible and, in some cases, is blatant heresy. For example, there are many Christians who absolutely love a book called *The Shack*, when in reality it teaches heresy concerning the Trinity. It's extremely vague and has an inadequate view of salvation. It essentially says that God has forgiven all people, but they might not know it. Not only that, but it has a distinctly unbiblical view of God's revelation and how He communicates today through His Word. It's a book filled with all kinds of theological errors, even though it may contain some biblical truth. And yet there are Christians who rave about it. That's an absolute lack of discernment.

Then there are Christians who love teachers like Joel Osteen, and before him, Robert Schuller—men who do not preach the Gospel. They never address the issue of man's sinfulness and his need to repent of his sin and turn to Christ to be his Savior from sin. In fact, I once spoke to a man who had followed Robert Schuller's ministry for years, and when I pointed certain matters out to him, he said, "Oh no, he's changed." No, he *hasn't* changed.

Then there's the attraction that many Christians have had over the years to the charismatic movement and its "health and wealth" preachers with their emphasis on supernatural miracles, healings, speaking in tongues, being healthy, being wealthy, extrabiblical revelation, female pastors, and some rather bizarre behavior like hysterical laughing—all in the name of Christianity. They see absolutely nothing wrong with those things.

Additionally, many believers have been drawn to "seeker-sensitive" churches and they don't even know it. The emphasis in those churches is not on exalting Christ by teaching what the Bible says, but rather on exalting man and on meeting people's personal desires or their perceived needs. It is a movement that caters to human interests instead of explaining what God has said in His Word, and the amazing thing about this is that some Christians in "seeker-sensitive" churches don't even realize that they're in those kinds of churches. That is to say, they don't discern the difference between a church that is founded on New Testament truth and principles and is Christ-centered, and a church that is, for the most part, man-centered. They're undiscerning and they don't even know it.

All that glitters is not gold, and some of the things that attract Christians these days are not from God. Therefore, you and I need to understand what the Bible has to say about discerning truth from error, because the amount of fool's gold, in the form of erroneous teaching, is only increasing. It's only getting worse, and we need to be equipped to handle it. It's important to understand what Scripture says about discernment so that we will not be deceived and fall into error. Those who never learn how to discern truth from error remain unstable in their Christian lives. They are up and down spiritually, all the time. They are constantly confused, not knowing who or what to believe. They're open to every religious trend and fad that comes down the road.

The apostle Paul compared Christians like this to naïve and gullible children because children will listen to anybody. They don't know the difference, and we adults understand that. That's completely normal, but there's a point when a person grows up from being a child. In Ephesians 4:11-13,

Paul talks about Christ giving men who teach the Word of God to the church. It says, *"And He gave some as apostles, and some as prophets, and some as evangelists, and some as pastors and teachers, for the equipping of the saints for the work of service, to the building up of the body of Christ; until we all attain to the unity of the faith, and of the knowledge of the Son of God, to a mature man, to the measure of the stature which belongs to the fullness of Christ."*

It's the Word of God that helps us to grow and mature to be more like Jesus Christ in character. If we don't do that, what happens? Ephesians 4:14-15 says, *"As a result, we are no longer to be children tossed here and there by waves, and carried about by every wind of doctrine, by the trickery of men, by craftiness and deceitful scheming; but speaking the truth in love, we are to grow up in all aspects into Him who is the Head, even Christ."* What Paul is saying is that those Christians who lack discernment are those Christians who don't grow spiritually like they should. Their spiritual growth is stunted. They fail to grow up to be like Christ because they do not listen to what the Word of God says.

I don't want any of you to be like that, so our study isextremely important. It focuses on this matter of spiritual discernment so that you can learn how to discern which speakers are from God, which books are written by men or women of God, and which are not.

The way John presents his teaching is by giving us three key truths about discerning truth from error. First of all, he tells us that we are commanded to test the spirits. This is not an option. This is a command. Second, John tells us the reason why we are to test the spirits. Why is it so important that we do this? Third, he explains the means by which we can test the spirits. How do you actually put them to the test? How do you know which are true and which are false? How can you discern?

As we begin our study of this passage, we want to look, at the first of these key truths about discerning truth from error—we are commanded to test the spirits. 1 John 4:1 begins this way, *"Beloved, do not believe every spirit, but test the spirits to see whether they are from God."* The first thing to understand about this statement is John's use of the term *spirit* or *spirits*. He tells us not to believe every spirit, but to *test* them. What does he mean by *spirit*? Why did he use this expression *spirit* rather than teacher? Notice the last sentence of chapter three; this is the connection. 1 John 3:24 says, *"The one who keeps His commandments abides in Him and He in him. We know by this that He abides in us, by the Spirit whom He has given us."* John speaks at the end of chapter three about the Holy Spirit whom God the Father gives to every Christian. All of us who know Christ have been given the Holy Spirit.

John moves on to what we identify as chapter four and speaks about those spirits who are not holy. That's the connection. He has spoken about the Spirit, who is the Holy Spirit. Now he moves on to speak about those spirits who are not holy. That is the connection here. By *spirit,* what John is referring to is the source of a teacher and his teaching. In other words, just as the Holy Spirit is the source of those who speak God's truth, so the devil is the source of those who teach error. In fact, he even mentions *"the spirit of the antichrist"* here. That would be devilish teaching.

Here's how one Bible teacher, John Stott, explains what the apostle John is saying. He writes, "True prophets are the mouthpiece of the Spirit of God, who, in verse six, is called the spirit of truth. False prophets are the mouthpiece of the spirit of error, or, as John tells us, the spirit of antichrist."[1] The apostle John is saying that behind every false teacher is the spirit of Satan, and that's why Christians need to be discerning. He's talking about the source, the origin of their message. Where does it come from? Does it come from the

Holy Spirit who is the third Person of the Trinity, or does it come from Satan and demons?

It is not always obvious when a teacher has Satan as the source of his message. If it were obvious, we would know it clearly, but it's not always that obvious. In 2 Corinthians 11:3, Paul said to the church that was so dear to him, *"But I am afraid that as the serpent"*—meaning Satan—*"deceived Eve by his craftiness, your minds will be led astray from the simplicity and purity of devotion to Christ."* False teachers had come into this church at Corinth, and they were influencing the people. They were telling the people that Paul was not a real apostle and that the message he preached was not from God, and they were corrupting this church. Now if you read verses 13-15, Paul clarifies what he means about Satan, or the serpent, corrupting and deceiving them. He says, *"For such men"*—now he's talking about those who had come in among the Corinthians—*"are false apostles, deceitful workers, disguising themselves as apostles of Christ. No wonder, for even Satan disguises himself as an angel of light. Therefore, it is not surprising if his servants also disguised themselves as servants of righteousness, whose end will be according to their deeds."* Paul is teaching that Satan's messengers, his prophets, his teachers are not always easy to identify because they are out to deceive us. Therefore, keep this in mind: If the church at Corinth had the apostle Paul as its founder, its spiritual father and mentor, its apostle and teacher, and yet they fell for teaching that was from Satan, then any of us can. If someone who was under Paul's teaching can be that deceived, then certainly you and I are not immune to deception.

So many Christians allow themselves to become enamored with certain teachers for all the wrong reasons. They are impressed by absolutely ridiculous things such as a man's eloquence and his speaking ability, his academic credentials, and even his physical appearance. You say, "No, that can't be." It can be, and it is! Do you realize that one of the things that these false apostles said about Paul was, "Look at the man, and listen to him! He can't compare to us." We don't know what Paul looked like, but he must not have been terribly attractive, and compared to these false apostles, his speech must not have been as eloquent as theirs because in 2 Corinthians 10:10, Paul tells us what they were saying about him. *"For they say, 'His letters are weighty and strong, but his personal presence unimpressive and his speech contemptible.'"* I doubt that Paul had contemptible speech, but, most likely, these men were extremely eloquent. We would probably say in our terminology that they spoke like Shakespearean actors compared to the apostle Paul, who probably just had a very normal voice and not, perhaps, a great deal of stage presence. That's what they were saying. "Yes, he writes to you like he's impressive, but when you see the guy, he's nothing to look at, and listen to the way he speaks." So the Corinthians were gravitating to these men for all the wrong reasons, and people do that today.

Now let's go back to 1 John. Notice what John specifically commands us to do. He commands us not to believe every spirit but rather, he tells us to *test* them in order to determine whether or not they are from God. First of all, I want you to realize that this statement from John is an apostolic command, which means it is a command from Jesus Christ through the pen of the apostle John. This is not an option that you can toss away and say, "Well, I don't really want to be discerning. I don't feel like being discerning. It sounds like a lot of work." You and I don't have an option, not if Christ is our Lord. He said, "This is a command."

Secondly, I want you to notice that this command is for every one of us, not simply for pastors and those who lead the church. Now it's true that pastors are called to protect their flocks by addressing error and teaching truth. That's why they need to be men who know the Word. When Paul tells Timothy and Titus that an elder must be *"able to teach"* (1 Timothy 3:2), he doesn't simply mean that he has to be willing to teach. Paul means that he has to have the spiritual ability to teach. He has to be gifted in that area. He has to know the Word of God. He has to be able to refute error. He has to be able to expound the Word of God. So it is true that pastors have to be especially discerning to protect their flocks.

It is also true that some Christians have been given a spiritual gift of discernment. In 1 Corinthians 12:10, Paul calls it the *"distinguishing of spirits."* So there are some who have been gifted to be very discerning when it comes to truth and error. However, what John is teaching us here is not about that at all. He's not talking about pastors. He's not talking about those who have been gifted in this area. He is saying that we as Christians are responsible before God to test each and every teacher to whom we listen to determine if they're from God or not, and you don't need a Bible college or a seminary degree to do this. You do need to listen carefully, and you do need to use your minds to evaluate what teachers are saying. In other words, we are called to be like the Bereans who, when Paul came to their town and started preaching Jesus to them, began *"examining the Scriptures daily"* (Acts 17:11) to see whether or not the things Paul was telling them were biblical or not. They didn't even listen to Paul unless they checked it out.

John has given us a command, a charge, not to believe every teacher we hear but to test them. What exactly does he mean by *test* them? The Greek word that is translated *test* could also be translated "examine." This particular word was used in ancient Greek literature to speak of coins that had been tested or examined to determine if the metals were pure and if they were of full weight and value, so that gives you an idea of what John is talking about. The clear command from John is that we are not to be gullible; we are not to be naïve; we are not to believe every religious teacher we hear, even if they use Bible verses. We are not to assume that just because they use Bible verses and mention the name Jesus, God's Spirit resides in them and is teaching through them. Instead, we are to test them to determine whether or not they are from God.

But why? Why is this so important for us? Why do we all need to be involved in this testing of spirits? John proceeds to tell us why in the last phrase of 1 John 4:1, as he gives us a second key truth about testing the spirits, which is the reason we're to test the spirits. John says. *"...because many false prophets have gone out into the world."* John is very clear. He plainly says it's so important that we examine every religious teacher, even those who claim to teach the Bible, because many false prophets have gone out into the world. The people who John was writing to had experienced this firsthand. John writes in 1 John 2:18-19, *"Children, it is the last hour and just as you heard that antichrist is coming"*—that's the one world ruler—*"but even now many antichrists"* —that is, those who have the same spirit of antichrist— "have *appeared. From this we know that this is the last hour. They went out from us,"* — meaning they left the church, — *"but they were not really of us, for if they had been of us,"* — meaning if they were truly saved, if they had really been converted— *"they would have remained with us."* They would have continued in our fellowship. They would have continued to embrace orthodox, biblical Christianity as taught by the apostles, but they went out so that it would be shown that they are not of us. They left the truth because they were never of the truth.

It is important to realize that John is not limiting these false prophets to this one church or to a handful of churches. His point is that Satan has sent his messengers into the whole world. They're everywhere, in many places. He's done this in order to deceive and mislead people with error, and it has only increased over time.

Where do you find these false prophets? Aside from some rather obvious false religions, they can be found within the sphere of Christendom in mainline denominations. They are in many seminaries, pulpits of liberal churches, and so-called Christian colleges and organizations. These false prophets also write books! They write books that appear in local Christian bookstores, because local Christian bookstores are not hotbeds of discernment. The way you get a book into a local Christian bookstore is you get a publisher that says it will make money for the bookstore. They're not discerning about such matters. If it sells, they'll put it in their stores.

They can also be seen on television and heard on radio, and they are not always so obvious because they mix truth with error. If they didn't do that, it would be very clear who they are. But because their message is a mixture of biblical truth and error rather than straightforward error, we have to examine them carefully.

There are schools today that were once biblically sound and orthodox, but now they're filled with teachers who deny the authority of Scripture and many of the essentials of the doctrine of our faith. There are cults and false religions that speak about Jesus and use a great deal of biblical terminology, but they're really led by false teachers. That shouldn't surprise us. The Bible tells us that this type of thing will happen, and it happened in the days of the apostles. Just look, for example, at Jude 4. *"For certain persons have crept in unnoticed."* — crept in where? Into our churches— *"those who were long ago before marked out for this condemnation, ungodly persons who turned the grace of our God into licentiousness and deny our only master and Lord Jesus Christ."* Essentially, what Jude is saying is they creep into our churches and they start teaching that you can live any way you want, that grace covers everything, and they deny the lordship, authority, and supremacy of God to rule over our lives. In 2 Peter 2:1, Peter says essentially the same thing: *"But false prophets also arose among the people"* — he's talking about in Old Testament times— *"just as there will also be false teachers among you, who will secretly introduce destructive heresies, even denying the master who bought them, bringing swift destruction upon themselves."*

Both Jude and Peter say that these false teachers will be among Christians, but in Acts 20:28, the apostle Paul said something that's frightening when speaking to the elders of the church at Ephesus. He said, *"Be on guard for yourselves and for all the flock among which the Holy Spirit has made you overseers, to shepherd the church of God which He purchased with His own blood."* He warns the elders to be on guard for themselves and for their flock. He says in verse 29, *"I know that after my departure savage wolves will come in among you, not sparing the flock."* What he means here is, "After I leave, after I pass from the scene, I know that there will be false teachers who will come in from the outside and they will hurt the flock." Come in where? Come into the church!

But notice verse 30, and this is what is most frightening. *"And from among your own selves men will arise, speaking perverse things to draw away the disciples after them."* Remember, he's talking to the elders of the church at Ephesus. *"From among your own selves..."* Do you mean, Paul, that there will be elders in our own church that will turn people towards heresy and to follow them rather than Christ? That's exactly what Paul means. The reason that the apostle John has commanded us to test the spirits of teachers is because false teachers are all around us, and you can't judge them by their appearance. You can't judge them by their speaking ability. That won't tell you if they're from God or not. They might look good, they might sound good, but, in reality, they might just be "fool's gold;" worthless iron pyrite rather than precious gold from God.

So, if we're commanded to test the spirits of the teachers, and the reason that we are to do this is because they are so many of them all around us, then how do we do it? How do we actually go about doing this? Are we to question every teacher before we listen to them? Do we give them a questionnaire? Do they have to pass an examination? In the next few verses John gives us several guidelines to help us in examining religious teachers as he gives us the third key truth about testing the spirits. He tells us the way to test the spirits in verse two: *"By this you know the Spirit of God: every spirit that confesses that Jesus Christ has come in the flesh is from God."*

The first thing that John tells us about how to determine if someone is a true or a false teacher is that you can know if the Spirit of God is speaking through a man if that man proclaims the truth about Jesus Christ. Now when John says, *"every spirit that confesses that Jesus Christ has come in the flesh,"* he means that this man proclaims in his message that Jesus Christ is God; God who took on flesh and became man. He is the incarnate deity, the God-man. You know that a man who teaches the truth about Christ's deity has the Spirit of God as the source of his message because this is what the Spirit of God teaches throughout the New Testament. John 1:1 says, *"In the beginning was the word, the word was with God, the word was God,"* and verse 14 says, *"The word dwelt among us, and we beheld his glory, glory as of the only begotten Son."* The Spirit of God teaches that Jesus Christ was in the beginning with God because He is God.

Paul taught this same truth in Colossians 2:9. He says, *"In him all the fullness of Deity dwells in bodily form."* This is precisely the truth with which John began his letter. First John 1:1-3 says, *"What was from the beginning, what we have heard, what we have seen with our eyes, what we have looked at and touched with our hands concerning the word of life, and the life was manifested, and we have seen and testified and proclaimed to you the eternal life which was with the Father and was manifested to us, what we have seen and heard, we proclaim to you that you, too, may have fellowship with us, and indeed our fellowship is with the Father and with His Son Jesus Christ."*

Once again, John Stott wrote these words: "It is understandable that the same Spirit through whom the miraculous conception took place should be our faithful witness to it."[2] Some of the false teachers and Gnostics of John's day specifically denied that Jesus Christ was God in human flesh. We know from historical records that there was a man in John's day, Cerinthus, who rose up and opposed John. He specifically separated Jesus from the Christ, teaching that something called the Christ-spirit came upon the man Jesus at his baptism, and then the Christ-spirit departed from this man Jesus just before his crucifixion.

Teachers from God don't teach that. They teach the truth about Jesus Christ; that He is fully divine and fully man. He is the second Person of the Trinity, the Son of God, and God the Son. Therefore, the way that you can test a speaker is to listen to what he has to say about Jesus, because all who speak by the Spirit of God confess that Jesus Christ is the God-man.

However, this confession that John is referring to is not simply recognition or even doctrinal acceptance of Christ's deity. It is certainly that, but it goes beyond that. The New Testament tells us that during Christ's earthly ministry, even demons recognized who He was, and they confessed that He was the Son of God. Demons have their theology right about Christ, so it has to mean more than that. James says that even the demons believe and they tremble (James 2:19). They confessed He was the Son of God, so to confess Christ as deity is more than just confessing an orthodox doctrinal position. It is to openly confess your personal faith and trust in Christ as Lord and Savior. The reason that God became a man in the

Person of Jesus Christ is so that He could die as the perfect substitute for sinners and call us to trust in that sacrificial death for our salvation. When we talk about the deity of Christ, we talk about the reason behind the deity. God became a man so that He could die for sinners; therefore, to confess Christ as God involves a belief that salvation is only by grace through faith in Christ and His atoning work. True teachers from God believe and teach this. They not only have an orthodox position of Christ's deity, but they also understand what the Cross is all about, which is tied to His deity.

Not only do true teachers teach the truth about Christ and salvation through Him, but they honor Him. They exalt Him as Lord because that is the ministry of the Holy Spirit. One of the ways that you know the charismatic movement, for the most part, is not of God is because, if the Spirit were in it, He would not be exalting Himself. He would be exalting Christ. Let me show you this in John 16. Jesus is teaching His disciples about what life will be like when He's gone, and He tells them about the coming of the Holy Spirit. He says in verses 13-14, *"But when he, the Spirit of truth comes, he will guide you into all the truth"* —this is a specific promise for the apostles, that He will guide them into writing the New Testament— *"for He will not speak on his own initiative but whatever he hears he will speak and he will disclose to you what is to come"* —that is, He will lead you into prophecy— *"He will glorify Me"* —that's the ministry of the Holy Spirit, to glorify Christ— *"for He will take of Mine and will disclose it to you."*

The New Testament is just that. It's the New Testament of Christ. It's all about Christ. John 16:15 says, *"All things that the Father has are Mine; therefore, I said that He takes of Mine and will disclose it to you."* The way to test a teacher is to listen to what he says about Christ. Not only does he believe in His deity, but does he exalt Him as God? Does he honor Him? Does he worship Him? Does he call you to surrender your life to Christ's Lordship? Does he glorify the

Son of God, or does he preach himself? Does he try to lead you to follow him?

A great verse in which Paul nails down how to discern whether someone is a man of God or a man of Satan is 2 Corinthians 4:5— *"For we do not preach ourselves, but Christ Jesus as Lord and ourselves as your bondservant for Jesus' sake."* True teachers don't exalt themselves; they exalt Christ. True teachers don't teach about themselves; they teach about Christ as Lord. True teachers recognize that they are simply bondservants to exalt Christ, to expose you to Jesus Christ.

If we can know that the Holy Spirit is behind a man's teaching based on his confession of Christ as the incarnate God and his attitude of exalting and glorifying the Lord, then it only makes sense that those who don't hold to this view of Christ must have the spirit of Satan behind them. That's precisely what John goes on to say in verse three, *"And every spirit that does not confess Jesus is not from God. This is the spirit of the antichrist of which you heard that it is coming, and now is already in the world."* What John is saying is that every teacher who denies the deity of Christ has, as the source of his ministry, the spirit of the antichrist. The Antichrist is that coming one-world ruler who will lead the nations against truth during the Tribulation period. He will oppose Christ. The Scripture says that He will oppose everything that is dear to the heart of Christ, specifically believers and Israel, and he will exalt himself as god. What John is saying is that the same satanic spirit that will inspire this coming man now inspires all false teachers. It is Satan's spirit, and you can identify false teachers by the fact that they do not believe or embrace Christ as God, nor do they teach that salvation is solely through faith in His shed blood.

This includes all cults, like Jehovah's Witnesses and Mormons, who very clearly deny the deity of Christ and salvation by Him alone. They say that's not true, but they're just trying to deceive you. That is true; they do not believe in Christ's deity. They do not believe that salvation comes through faith in Him and His atoning work on the Cross alone. This also includes any teacher who doesn't teach the truth about Christ, even though they may speak a great deal about the Bible and they may wow you with their dynamic personality. John tells us not to be naïve. That person has the spirit of antichrist behind him, and you can know it by what he says and believes concerning Jesus.

There are other guidelines that John gives us, but I want to impress upon you to listen with discernment. When you hear a message, when you read a book, be discerning. What is this individual saying about Jesus and salvation? Forget about the charismatic personality of the individual. Forget about the man's speaking ability or his appearance or his charm or his writing ability. What does he say about Christ and salvation? That's where it begins, and that's where it ends. Follow what John says here, and you'll see right through books like *The Shack*, speakers like Joel Osteen, movements that aren't biblical, and on and on it goes. Otherwise, you will not have a clue as which teachers to believe, who to read, and what to embrace, and you'll be tossed about by every wind of doctrine.

The question that I leave with you is this: Do you personally know the truth about Jesus Christ? Have you personally trusted Him as your Lord and Savior, or do you just have an orthodox view about Him? Now you ought to have an orthodox view about Him, but it's not just head knowledge. It's not just that you know the truth about Him. Have you ever personally trusted Him as the One dying on the Cross for you? That is what the Bible refers to as the message of salvation. He died for sinners like us. When you believe that and you are ready to forsake your sin of running your own life, when you turn to Christ to trust Him as the One who forgives you through His shed blood, when you want Him to run your life and reign over you, that's what it means to become a Christian. Make sure that you've repented. Make sure that you've trusted Him to save you, and once you do that, then you embrace this truth, and you become discerning as you listen to other speakers. Let's pray.

Father, I thank You that this is in Your Word. I thank You, Lord, that we don't have to lack discernment.

Father, You know that my heart is burdened that the people who attend this church might be discerning. How it saddens my heart and the hearts of our other leaders to hear that some of our people sit here under the teaching of the Word for years and yet seem to lack any kind of discernment about false teachers. I pray that You'll help us, Lord, to test the spirits, to believe that which needs to be believed and which is clearly from You, and not to believe that which is clearly not from You. May we be discerning not only about teachers we listen to, but also the books we read. Lord, help us to embrace, follow, and apply what John has to say here in this letter.

I pray that You will protect our church so that we might be a place where our leaders are always men of the Word, men of God who do not promote themselves. But Lord, we want to preach Jesus Christ alone, and by your strength we'll continue to do that. We pray all this in Jesus' name, Amen.

---

[1]Stott, John R. W.*The Letters of John*. Carol Stream, IL: Tyndale House Publishers, 1998. 153.

[2]Ibid.